EVERYWOMAN

Edited by Gina Luria

Jane Austen Sisters
Female Education
Mary Wollstonecraft

Also by Virginia Tiger

William Golding:
The Dark Fields of Discovery

EVERYWOMAN

by Gina Luria and Virginia Tiger

DESIGN BY
Harriett Banner

RANDOM HOUSE  NEW YORK

All rights reserved under International and Pan-American Copyright Conventions. Published in the United States by Random House, Inc., New York, and simultaneously in Canada by Random House of Canada Limited, Toronto.

Library of Congress Cataloging in Publication Data
Luria, Gina, 1942–
    Everywoman.

     1. Women—Psychology.   2. Sex role.   3. Women—Social conditions.   4. Women—Poetry.
I. Tiger, Virginia, joint author.   II. Title.
HQ1206.L88   301.41'2
76-14188
ISBN 0-394-49782-1
ISBN 0-394-73245-6 pbk.

Manufactured in the United States of America
9 8 7 6 5 4 3 2
First Edition

Grateful acknowledgment is made to the following for permission to reprint previously published material:

Mr. Chris Albertson: Photograph of Bessie Smith by Carl Van Vechten (p. 106).

The American Federation of the Arts: "A Ceremonial at a Young Ladies' Seminary" by an unknown artist c. 1810 (p. 72) from the Collection of Edgar William and Bernice Chrysler Garbisch.

Ashmolean Museum, Oxford: Picture of Queen Elizabeth I (p. 114).

Bantam Books, Inc.: Excerpt from "Paphnutius" by Hrotsvitha, translated by Sister Mary Marguerite Butler, R.S.M. Reprinted from *Medieval and Tudor Drama* (Gassner). Copyright © 1963 by Bantam Books, Inc.

Ms. Sharon Barba: "The Cycle of Women" by Sharon Barba from *Best Friends and Rising Tides*. Copyright © 1973 by Sharon Barba (Simon & Schuster).

Geoffrey Brereton: Excerpt from "Little Red Riding Hood" translated by Geoffrey Brereton from *The Fairy Tales of Charles Perrault*.

Jovanna Ceccarelli, Publisher, *Theatre Arts*: Drawing by Charles Baskerville, Jr. from the cover of *Theatre Arts Magazine*, September 1923.

Chappell-Morris Limited: Four lines of lyrics from "Ugly Duckling" c. & a. by Frank Loesser. Copyright 1951 by Frank Loesser. Original Publisher Frank Music Corp.

Carol Donner: Illustrations on p. 95 reprinted from *Body Sculpture* by Simona Morini (Delacorte Press) courtesy of the illustrator, Carol Donner.

Editions E. De Boccard: Print entitled "La Comparison" by F. Janinet, (p. 94).

Norma Millay Ellis, Literary Executor of the Estate of Edna St. Vincent Millay: Two poems "The Concert" and "Sonnet xli, "I being born a woman and distressed" from *Collected Poems*, Harper & Row. Copyright 1923, 1934, 1951, 1962 by Edna St. Vincent Millay and Norma Millay Ellis.

Escher Foundation: Woodcut of "Witch" 1931 (p. 16). Escher Foundation-Haags Gemeentemuseum, The Hague, Holland.

Esquire: Illustration entitled "July, 1950" from calendar by Al Moore. Copyright 1949 by Esquire Inc., (p. 86).

Farrar, Straus & Giroux, Inc.: "The Crown" and "Women" from *The Blue Estuaries* by Louise Bogan. Copyright 1923, 1929, 1930, 1931, 1933, 1934, 1935, 1936, 1937, 1938, 1941, 1951, 1952, 1954, © 1968 by Louise Bogan.

W. H. Freeman and Company Publishers: Brief excerpt from "Immunization against Smallpox before Jenner" by William L. Langer, January, 1976. Copyright © 1976 by Scientific American, Inc.

Galleria Degli Uffizi: Painting by Lorenzo Lippi entitled "St. Agatha offering her abated breasts to God…" (p. 117).

Girl Talk: Excerpt from "Baby You're Beautiful…" *Girl Talk*, 1975.

Harcourt Brace Jovanovich, Inc.: Excerpt from *The Waste Land* by T. S. Eliot.

Harper's Magazine: Excerpt from Josephine Hendin interview, "Doris Lessing: The Phoenix Midst Her Fifties" from *Harper's* July 1973. Copyright © 1973 by Harper's Magazine.

William Heinemann Medical Books, Ltd.: Illustration of Iron Chastity Belt reprinted from *Woman* (1927), Ploss, Bartels and Bartels, (p. 25).

Houghton Mifflin Company: Eight lines from "The Sisters" from *The Complete Poetical Works of Amy Lowell*. Copyright © 1955 by Houghton Mifflin Company. Also, six lines from "The Operation" from *All My Pretty Ones* by Anne Sexton. Copyright © 1961, 1962 by Anne Sexton.

Human Behavior Magazine: Excerpt from "Violence in the Children's Room" by Wayne Sage, December, 1975. Copyright © 1975 by *Human Behavior* Magazine.

Henry E. Huntington Library and Art Gallery: Photograph of Thomas Gainsborough painting "Lady with a Spaniel" (p. 77).

Irving Berlin Music Corporation: Excerpt from "You Can Have Him" by Irving Berlin at p. 42. Copyright © 1949 by Irving Berlin. Reprinted by permission. All rights reserved.

Alexander Laing. Administrator of the estate of Dilys Laing: Poem entitled "Veterans" from *By a Woman Writt*, (Goulianos) Bobbs-Merrill, 1973.

Mr. Christopher Lasch: Excerpt from "Better Than to Burn…" published in *The Forum*, Volume II, No. 4 (Fall, 1973).

Mme. A. Lejard: Print entitled "Beauty" from *La Femme & L'Amour* by André Lejard, Editions Albin Michel, 1946 (p. 84).

Ms. Estelle Leontief: Pictures of Pompeii.

Liberation Magazine: "The Education of Women" by Florence Howe. Copyright © 1969 by Liberation Magazine, 339 Lafayette St., N.Y., N.Y.

Macmillan Publishing Co., Inc.: Three poems "When You Are Old," Copyright 1906 by Macmillan Publishing Co., Inc. and renewed 1934 by William Butler Yeats; "Prayer for my Daughter," Copyright 1924 by Macmillan Publishing Co., Inc. and renewed 1952 by Bertha Georgie Yeats; and "Adam's Curse" all reprinted from *Collected Poems of William Butler Yeats*. Also, the illustration "De Conceptu" (Birth Scene) on p. 11 by Jacob Ruefls reprinted from Volume I, *Greek and Roman*, by W. S. Fox, which is a part of the thirteen-volume publication *The Mythology of All Races*, by L. H. Gray.

Magnum Photos, Inc.: Photographs on p. 159 by Cornell Capa; on p. 160, clockwise from top left, by Charles Harbutt, Jill Freedman, Sergio Larrain, Richard Kalvar, Sergio Larrain, David Seymour, Burk Uzzle, Charles Harbutt (photo in center also by Charles Harbutt); on pp. 162-163 by Charles Harbutt.

The Mansell Collection: Print entitled "Witch on a Broomstick" (p 17).

Mercedes Music Co.: Six lines of lyrics from "Don't Answer The Door" by Jimmy Johnson. Used by permission of the copyright owner Mercedes Music Co.

The Metropolitan Museum of Art: Flemish painting by Rogier van der Weyden, 'Workshop of the Nativity' —left wing, *The Visitation*. The Metropolitan Museum of Art, Purchase, 1949, The Cloisters Collection. (p. 8).

Ms. Josephine Miles: "Sale" by Josephine Miles from *Prefabrications*, Indiana University Press, 1956.

The Museum of Modern Art: 'Cyclops,' Plate III by Odilon Redon. From the portfolio Origines (1883). Lith-

ACKNOWLEDGMENTS

A book as wide-ranging as ours demands eclectic contributions. We were the finders and keepers of much generous wisdom and aid. First, we wish to thank Barbara DiBlasi and Roberta Shortal who were throughout the writing of this book the vivid examples of our experience of the community of women as they helped us sew the seams of daily life.

We are grateful to, among others: Steven M. L. Aronson, Marie Collins, Mr. and Mrs. Gordon Conner, Leo and Jilly Cooper, Liz Darhansoff, Cory Deren, the DiBlasi family, Nancy Farrell, Doucet Devon Fischer, Alice Fredman, Eileen Green, Alex Greer, Suzanne Grossmann, Ann Hollander, George Horton, Ethel Kahn, Samuel and Rosalind Lourie, Ronnie Meyerson, Ruth Moulton, Lynn Nesbitt, Susan Piro, Blossom Primer, Karyl Roosevelt, Virginia Rouslin, Jack Schor, Annamay Sheppard, Babs Simpson, Cris Sosnowski, Erica Spellman, Susan Starr, Lionel Tiger, Agnes Timar, Beatrice Waldbaum, Maryann Wasik, our students in the Women's Studies Program at Rutgers-Newark.

We wish to thank especially the abundant efforts and support of both Mr. Gil Cohen and Mr. James Merritt at the Dana Library of Rutgers University–Newark, as well as the staffs of the Cornell Medical School Library, the Frick Collection Library, the British Museum, the New-York Historical Society, the Newark Public Library, and the New York Public Library.

This book is not a catalog of Learned Ladies; we were never solely interested in historical superstars. Yet, for us, there is one Learned Lady who emerges from the galaxy of women as a luminary. It has been our fortune to create this book under her light. And we wish to thank her, Toni Morrison, our editor.

To Lionel

V.

To Richard
and the memory of my mother

G.

CONTENTS

EVERYWOMAN

Women have no wilderness in them
They are provident instead,
Content in the tight hot cell of their hearts
To eat dusty bread.

. . .

They wait, when they should turn to journeys
They stiffen, when they should bend
They use against themselves that benevolence
To which no man is friend.

. . .

They hear in every whisper that speaks to them
A shout and a cry.
As like as not, when they take life over their door-sills
They should let it go by.

"Women," Louise Bogan

I dared—
It was not God's proclamation.

—Antigone

Memories of the Flesh

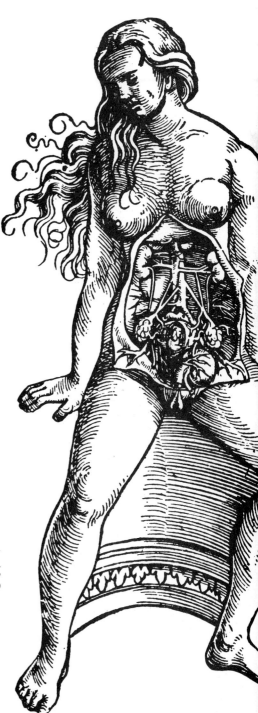

WOMEN bear children. This moment, in America alone, eight women have just given birth. It takes time. It hurts and women die; children too. Midwives help or hinder. Doctors heal or wound. Puerperal fever, Caesarean incision, abortion, episiotomy, breech birth: the gigantical thrust of the skull as the vaginal lips open. But women do it, have done it and will do it.

Like so many other things in women's diurnal life: motherhood, warfare, courtship, education, philanthropy—labor has a history. The history of childbirth has been experience. Some men have drawn it, painted it, but only women know about it, know that its triumph is not confined to the private province of the lying-in chamber.

Cave drawings of 40,000 B.C. reveal the first representations of the human body. In A.D. 1500 the first observation and description of the internal human anatomy is made. That span of 41,000 years marks the beginning of the perpetual lag between advances in technology and the use of these advances to improve the texture of human life. So women, ignorant of their interiors, continue to have babies. Men and women continue to observe rituals, creeds, myths.

> I will greatly multiply thy sorrow and thy conception; in sorrow thou shalt bring forth children; and thy desire shall be to thy husband and he shall rule over thee.
> —*Genesis*

The mother-womb is monster or wonder.

Grande Pueblos

To be sung by the one who first takes
the child from its mother
Newborn, on the naked sand
Nakedly lay it.
Next to the earth mother,
That it may know her;
Having good thoughts of her, the food giver.
Newborn, we tenderly
In our arms take it,
Making good thoughts.
House-god, be entreated,
That it may grow from childhood to man-
    hood,
Happy, contented;
Beautifully walking
The trail to old age.
Having good thoughts of the earth its
    mother,
That she may give it the fruits of her being.
Newborn, on the naked sand
Naked lay it.

—Mary Austin, "Song to the Newborn," 1928

IN THE sixteenth century the skilled anatomist Andreas Vesalius and his illustrator, Jan Keller, map in *De humani corporis fabrica* the terrain of woman's fabulous womb. But minute and faithful reproductions of woman's insides don't change the lives of women bearing children. For two hundred years men split pubic hairs over the exact configuration of the uterus, the vaginal canal, the pudendum, the os pubis. Chauliac, famous French surgeon of the early fourteenth century, says:

> The uterus is like a penis turned inside out . . . it has in its upper part two arms with testicles . . . like the scrotum . . . a common body in the middle . . . a column with a canal in it like the shaft . . . and the vulva is like glans and preputium.

WILLIAM HARVEY (who is remembered as the discoverer of the blood's circulation but is almost unknown as the father of British midwifery) transforms the lives of women by marrying the precise work of Vesalius with his own observation of women in labor. With

Ancient Indian practice of speeding labor by having brave run on horseback toward woman

method and accuracy he describes the anatomical structure and functions of female organs in *De generatione animalium*, 1651:

> Various, then, is the constitution of the uterus, and not only in its diseased but also in its natural state, that is, at the periods of fecundity and barrenness. In young girls . . . and in women past child-bearing, it is without blood and about the size of a bean. In the marriageable virgin it has the magnitude and form of a pear. In women who have borne children, and are still fruitful, it equals in build a small gourd or a goose's egg; at the same time, together with the breasts, it swells and softens, becomes more fleshy, and its heat is increased, whilst to use Virgil's expression with reference to the fields "Superat tener omnibus humor/Et genitalia semina poscunt."
>
> Wherefore women are most prone to conceive either just before or just subsequent to menstrual flux, for at these periods there is a greater degree of heat and moisture, two conditions necessary to generation. In the same manner, when other animals are in heat the genital organs are moist and turgid. Such is the state of the uterus as I have found it before birth.

AND *De partu*, Harvey's chapter on labor, is the first original treatise on midwifery by an English author. "Nature," he writes, "must be our adviser, the paths she chalks must be our

"Le Toucher" (the toucher). Artist's representation of a gynecological examination

Maternity girdles

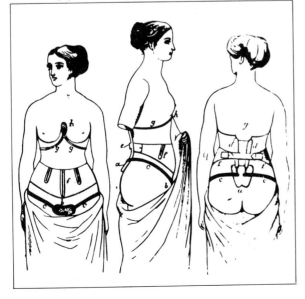

walk. Nature is the perfect midwife, none of whose works are made in vain but all directed to some end and some good."

Slowly, men from the public world of learning begin to attend to the matrix of life: they bring their black bags—their first tools are observation, deduction, and experimentation. Later they devise forceps, "delivery beds," anesthetics, curettes, specula, examining chairs, and rabbit tests (a major breakthrough in 1931). Gradually there emerges a science of obstetrics.

Like all intrusions of men into woman's sphere, their presence brings pain and confusion as well as release and pleasure. In the late seventeenth century male doctors replace female midwives; lying-in hospitals replace private birth chambers. Frequent internal examinations of pregnant women represent a vital advance in obstetrical technique. A consequence of this is that women die by the thousands in epidemics of puerperal fever. Ignorant that they are passing pestilent infection from the dead and dying to the living and well (the mother and her fetus), doctors become the agents of fatal disease. Alexander Gordon, a Scots physician, speculates about the role of the doctor in the transmission of disease:

> This disease seized such women, only as were visited, or delivered by a practitioner, who had previously attended patients affected with the disease . . . I had evident proofs that every person, who had been with a patient in the Puerperal Fever, became charged with an atmosphere of infection which was communicated to every pregnant woman, who happened to come within its sphere . . . It is a disagreeable declaration for me to mention, that I myself was the means of carrying the infection to a great number of women.

> —*A Treatise on the Epidemic Puerperal Fever of Aberdeen*, 1795

SOME MALE practitioners of obstetrics were trained by midwives like Mrs. Jane Sharp, author of *The Midwives Book, or the Whole Art of Midwifery Discovered: Directing Child-Bearing Women how to Behave Themselves in the Conception Breeding, and Nursing of Children* (1677). But when these men intruded on what was regarded as woman's domain, they were heatedly ridiculed.

> Such a man ought to be treated with as much indignity, as if he undertook to clear starch, hem a ruffle, or make a bed; yea, and with much greater; because in all these he is not called to handle the sacred parts of other men's wives . . . man-midwifery is a personal, a domestic, and a national evil.

> —John Blount, *Man-Midwifery Dissected*, 1793

A woman in the pain of childbirth

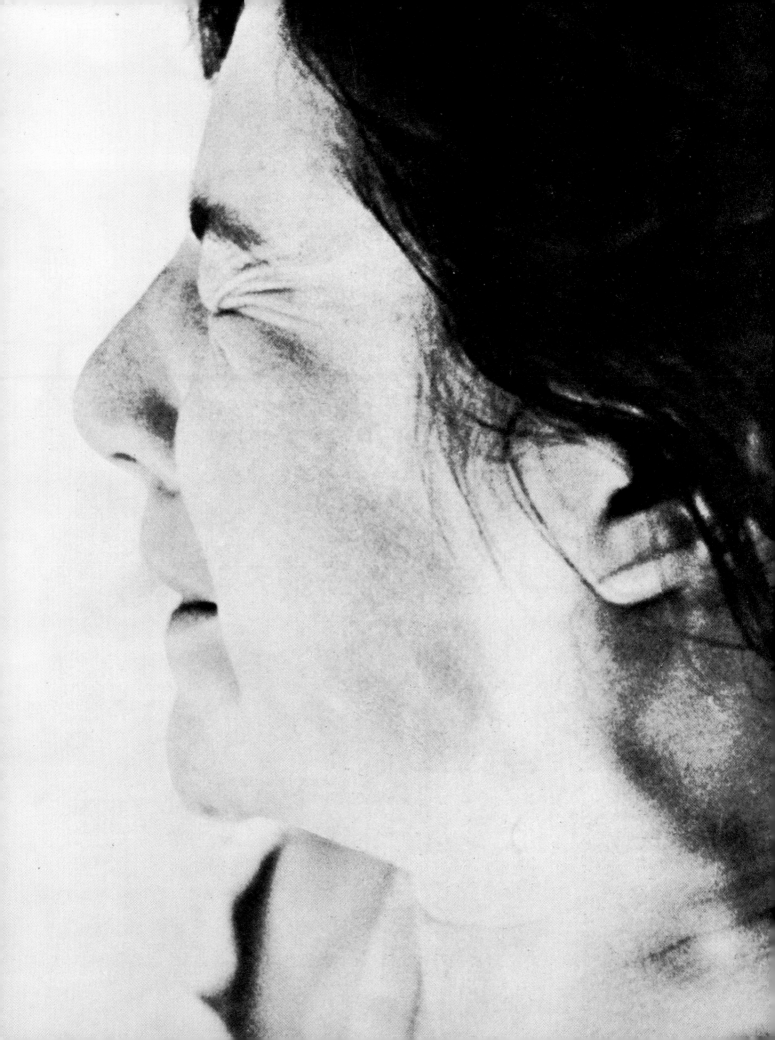

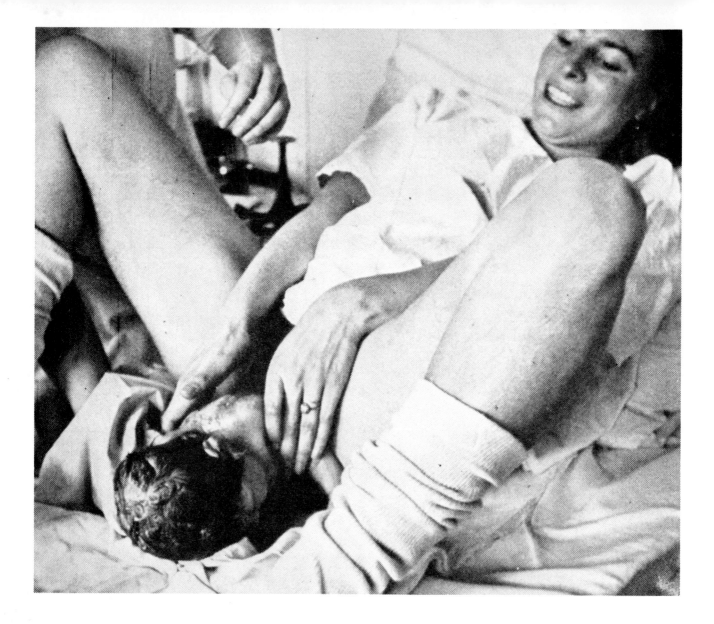

In fact, one of the most acrimonious skirmishes in the long battle of the sexes was waged over the man-midwifery question. There were many polemical broadsheets written by both men and women.

JUST as she discovers she is with child by observing the changes in her body—the ceasing of the menstrual flow, the blue dappling of the breasts—so she turns to the community of women who continue to cling to woman's lore rather than man's learning. As constant as the advances of medical technology is the habit of women calling upon each other to educate themselves in the necessities of birth and child care: old wives' tales and up-to-date fads from that parade of well-wishers—aunts, cousins, friends—bearing flowers, candy, movie magazines, multiple copies of Dr. Spock's book on child care, baby albums silky pink or blue. The wild rigmarole of ADVICE:

> "And listen, don't let him near you for four months; Charlie did, and he ruined my insides."

I can't help it, she said, pulling a long face,
It's them pills I took, to bring it off, she said.
(She's had five already, and nearly died of young George.)
The chemist said it would be all right, but I've never been the same.
You are a proper fool, I said.
Well, if Albert won't leave you alone, there it is, I said,
What you get married for if you don't want children?
HURRY UP PLEASE IT'S TIME

—T. S. Eliot, *The Waste Land*, 1922

CHILDBIRTH is the biological Works and Days of woman. Women live within the magic circle of necessity; they conceive; they gestate, they bear a child. They bear as well the terrors of childbirth:

fear of death
fear of begetting a monster
fear of those in attendance
fear of the body's permanent stretch
     and ruin
fear of pain

Pearl Buck's *The Good Earth* to the contrary, no one can say it doesn't hurt. There are approaches to pain, the Lamaze Method or totemic birth dolls. They are only two among many kinds of comfort.

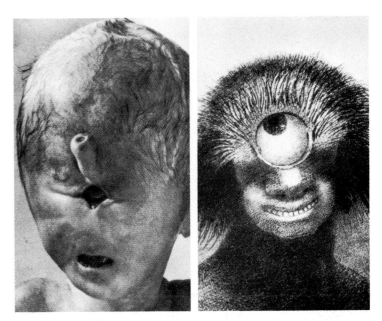

Real human cyclops and imaginary one

THE COMMUNITY of women is seen most vividly in the midwives at work.

As old as civilization is the history of midwifery. In every age and culture special attendants have proffered aid to the woman in labor, assuaging her pain, assisting her delivery, and tending her newborn. Reserved by tradition to females, the role of birth helper was known in English as *midwife* (with women), in French as *sage-femme* (wise woman). . . . The view of Roderigo a Castro, expressed in 1594, was prevalent until the eighteenth century: *Haec ars viros dedacet* (This art is not suitable for men). Physicians considered care of the parturient beneath their dignity.

—Harold Speert,
The Midwife in America, 1968

Yet, from the belly, from the bed, from the crib issues joy.

Away in a manger
A crib for a bed
The little lord Jesus
Laid down his sweet head
The Star in the bright sky
Looked down where he lay
The little lord Jesus
Asleep in the hay.

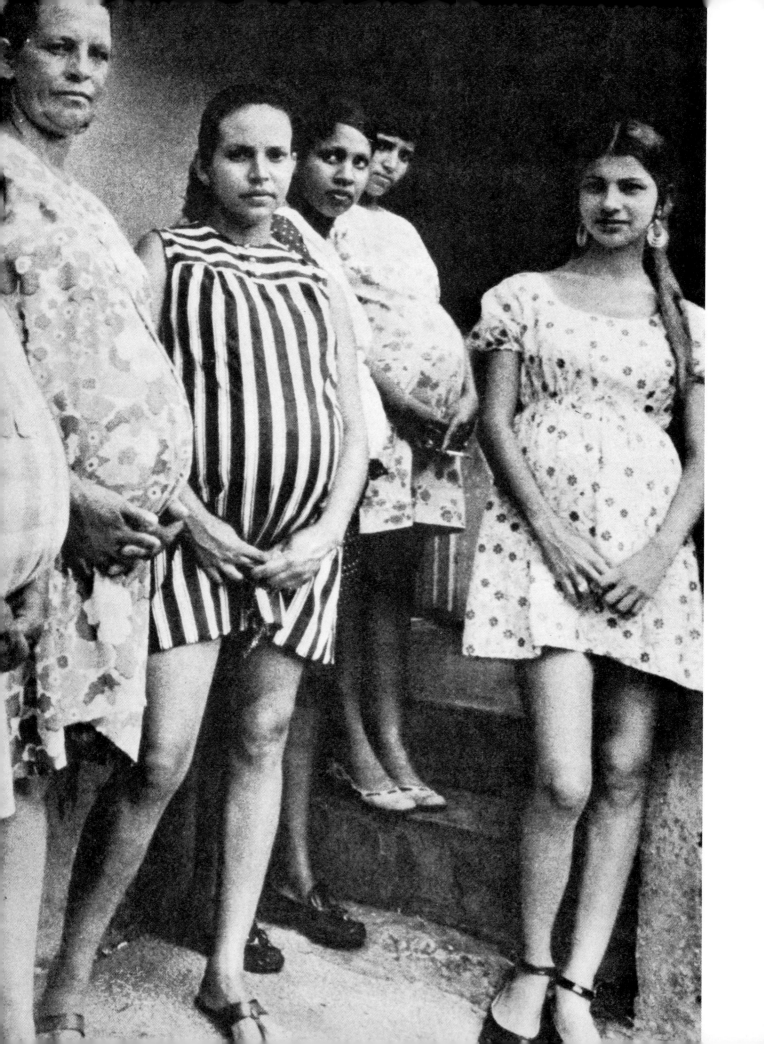

It must have been the second one because I was still living in Brooklyn; I was in the supermarket and the water burst I laughed so hard I thought I'd die and a nice woman took me home but before Bob and the ambulence could come the baby was coming out and the girl from downstairs came running up and I started screaming and she fainted and Bob walked in and stepped over her and I screamed – it's here! – and he caught it and dumped it on my stomach. And that was the way Scott was born.

VIOLENCE

The Wars of Women

Once I had a scolding wife
She wasn't very civil
I clapped a plaster on her mouth
And sent her to the Devil.

　　　　　—"Haul Away Joe,"
　　　American whaling ballad

Hyena Hag

Gürtelringkampf in der Schaubude. "Feste Wilhelm – Deutschlands Eiche!"

THE violence of women, singly and in groups, is one of the world's best-kept secrets. Tradition tells us that females are creatures of appealing passivity: sugar and spice and everything nice. But that's not what all little girls are made of. In our daily lives we know woman to be belligerent. Frying pan in hand, she intimidates, strikes out, but—it is believed—seldom kills. For the real threat which women hold is the secretiveness of their violence. So when in the wrestling ring or at the roller derby we see women openly displaying their talent for violence, we squirm in our seats, we smirk.

Woman's secretiveness has always been feared. Woman says to man:

> Stolen waters are sweet,
> and bread eaten in secret is pleasant.
> But [man] knoweth not that the dead are there;
> And that [woman's] guests are in the depths of hell.

> —Proverbs 9:13-18

WHEN we think of violent women we picture the witch, the poisoner, the blackmailer, the murderess, the castrator, the hyena hag. In these guises women are both frightening and erotic.

> All witchcraft comes from carnal lust, which is in women insatiable. . . . Wherefore for the sake of fulfilling their lusts they consort even with devils.

> —*The Witches' Hammer*, 1487

JUST the whisper of violence in women kindles suspicion and repression. In turn, if suspected of violence, women are always punished for sex, by sex, and with sex.

> Among the Puritans, no spirit of chivalry prevailed. The Massachusetts colony had a law that women suspected of witchcraft be stripped and their bodies scrutinized by a male "witch-pricker" to see if there was not the devil's mark upon them.

> —Calhoun, *Social History of the American Family*, 1922

IN FACT, there is evidence for the fantasies and fears. Women are the poisoners of the world: the annals of crime are filled with accounts of women who did not see their murders as unusual or wrong. One poison-ess said her activity was "ordinary enough business"; "poison appeared as her last, most faithful friend." Another woman retaliated against her lover's unfaithfulness by ripping off his penis. Even more common are women's maternal crimes—they beat babies:

> There were the children—a two-year-old baby strangled to death by her mother who forced black pepper down the girl's throat and into her windpipe; an 11-year-old girl starved to a weight of 31 pounds, deformed and retarded since age five from beatings . . . other children less than three years old beaten, burned, and suffocated.

> —Wayne Sage, "Violence in the Children's Room," *Human Behavior* (1975)

WOMEN "farm"—or neglect children; they blackmail; shoplift; commit the murder of husbands and lovers; tell false fortunes; lie, cheat, steal, dissemble. And her ability to pretend, to disguise her capacity for violence, triggers our prurient anxiety that woman may well be endlessly violent. Remember that men pay to see, as she strips, the she-devil, with whip. Men's dreams are clotted—so they tell us—with the toothed vagina, the black-booted temptress, the amazon, the sorceress with wiles. What we feel about this masked violence is excited, atavistic, mindless—as taboo-ridden, for both men and women, as the sight of menstrual blood.

> Women are natural guerrillas. Scheming, we nestle into the enemy's bed, avoiding open warfare, watching options, playing the odds. High, and made paranoiac by his observance of my rage, my husband has the fantasy of woman with a knife.
>
> —Sally Kempton, "Cutting Loose," 1970

OFTEN men and women come to blows. And in these bloody battles between the sexes, women always lose. Physically their bodies are simply too weak for masculine combat and conquest. The secret of their style of violence lies in their use of their sex.

> Women receive
> The insults of men
> With tolerance,
> having been bitten
> in the nipple
> by their toothless gums.
>
> —Dilys Laing, "Veterans," 1942

WE KNOW women can be menacing and powerful. To overcome might, women win by wiles. Women's hips are wider than men's, stronger too, for birth. These same hips can deal dirt and death. Women's power, which, like violence, they have in abundance, lies in the blood, in the bed, in the soup, in the claw, fang, shriek, screech, in the hoot of derision.
Woman is dangerous.

Jean Livingston, Good wife of Warriston, Stands Accused of Devizing her Husband's Murder.

Having conceived a deadly rancour, hatred and malice against John Kincaid of Warriston, for the alleged biting of her in the arme, and striking her divers times, the said Jean, in the month of June, one thousand six hundred years, directed Janet Murdo, her nurse, to the said Robert to the abbey of Holyroodhouse . . . to speak with her, anent the cruel and unnatural taking away of her said husband's life.

—Victor MacClure,
She Stands Accused, 1935

THE GOOD WIFE cunningly turns wicked witch, harpy, harridan, virago, scold, nag. Proverbs says: "It is better to dwell in a corner of the house top/than with a brawling woman in a wide house. It is better to dwell in the wilderness/than with a contentious and angry woman." And such a woman must be punished.

Here is an example to every good woman that she suffer and endure patiently, nor strive with her husband nor answer him before strangers, as did once a woman who did answer her husband before strangers with short words and he smote her in her visage and brake her nose, and all her life after she had her nose crooked, the which so shent and disfigured her visage after, that she might not for shame show her face, it was so foul blemished.

—Geoffrey de La Tour de Landry, *Book of the Knight of the Tower*, 1371

WHEN woman stands accused, she is ever after guilty, never again innocent.

Do you not know that you are each an Eve? You are the Devil's gateway.

—Tertullian

NO ONE is immune from this ancient view: our belief in the witch leagued with the devil is not a relic from some murky past. We still fear that the same sorcery emanates now from that most despised of creatures, the woman prisoner. In the female felon the witch once again stands accused, guilty—

Women of the Manson family

Medieval cartoon of the daughters of Danaus slaying their husbands

"Have you people got any .38 cartridges?"

"Silly woman! What have you done?"

hunted from hole to hole as if she was a beast of prey, or as if infected with a moral plague.

—Mary Wollstonecraft, *The Wrongs of Woman*, 1797

Mr. Alligood had been stabbed 11 times with an icepick he kept in a desk drawer; the fatal wound was in his heart. Missing from her cell, where the jailer was found dead last August, was 20-year old Joanne Little, a black woman who had been held in the jail for three months pending an appeal of her conviction on a charge of breaking and entering and burglary . . .

Subsequent disclosures in a medical examiner's report . . . and Miss Little's giving herself up and pleading self-defense, have turned the case into something far more complex, raising allegations about what goes on in small town jails and stirring demands for a Federal inquiry.

—*The New York Times*, December 1, 1974

ACCUSED then, the she-devil awaits judgment. Condemned before trial for having revealed, if only by hearsay, her propensity for *human* violence, her living prison is sexual shame.

Then the steward took her by the hand . . . and spoke many foul bawdy words unto her, purposing and desiring, as it seemed to her, to oppress her and ravish her. And then she had much dread. . . . "Sir, for the reverence of Almighty God, spare me for I am a man's wife." Then said the steward: "Thou shalt tell me whether thou hast this speech of God or the devil, or else thou shalt go to prison."
"Sir," said she, "to go to prison, I am not afraid for My Lord's love."
The steward, seeing her boldness in that she dreaded no prisoning, struggled with her, shewing unclean tokens and ungodly countenance. . . . "Either thou art a right good woman or else a right wicked one" and delivered her again to her jailer.

—Margery Kempe, *The Book of Margery Kemp*, fourteenth century

AMPLE as the evidence of women's capacity for violence is, it is remarkable how honorably women have controlled the exercise of that violence. We all know of centuries of abuse, of dismissal, of degradation, endured by women because of their sex. There is, sadly, a history of ignoble acts inflicted upon women because they are women. Consider that what may be the last witch-burning in the civilized world—in Peru, in 1888—is really not an isolated incident but just one example of that violent treatment of women which is an important part of women's history. And the scourging of witches is no more bizarre, spectacular, or forbidden than are those practices to prevent unlawful sexual intercourse—the pudential shield, infibulation, the chastity belt. Infibulation is particularly grisly:

The great labia on their internal surface are scraped with a razor, and then there is placed in the urethra a small funnel like a catheter for draining off the urine; thereafter, the feet are bound together, and from the malleoli up there is a regular bandaging continuing to the middle of the thighs so close together that the greater labie will come to adhere together. For eight days the patient must remain lying down, after which

Are You a Feminist?

Do you believe in the recall of babies?
In the ultimate elimination of the male?
Are you concerned about the Woman Problem?
Do you sew on your own buttons and cook your own meals?
Or are you a beautiful woman?
These absorbing questions and others will all be answered in the Feminist Number of Life which is coming just in time to give you the opportunity to become a regular subscriber, if you obey that impulse now.

the girls are permitted to rise; but for eight days more they must keep their feet and thighs close together so that the labie will not tear apart. When the operation has healed there remains but a small orifice for the draining of the urine and the menstrual fluid, . . .

> —Paolo Mantegazza, nineteenth-century account of infibulation, in *Sexual Relations of Mankind*

RAPE, of course, is an eternal constant for women.

So there is wisdom in woman's tactics: abstinence, evasion, silence. Subterfuge is a way of survival.

White women from Boston to Birmingham have shown themselves capable of stoning black children; recent mob riots and terrorist groups have included women of all races. Nevertheless, because the culture has been primarily *man*-made, and because women have been inheritors rather than inventors of its values, most of us have been only spectators to its violent traditions.

> —Letty Cottin Pogrebin, *Ms.*, 1975

> I like it here just fine
> and I don't want no bail
> My sister's here
> my mother's here
> and all my girlfriends too.
> I want my rights
> I'm fighting for my rights
> I want to be treated
> Just like *anybody* else
> I want to be treated
> Just like *everybody* else.
> *I like it fine in Jail*
> *And I don't want no Bail.*

> —Margaret Walker, "Girl Held Without Bail," 1964

WHEN provoked, men twist rancor into fists, guns, war. When provoked, women seem to hate in private silence. They give the appearance of submission, control, containment, calmness, endurance. They don't seem to thirst for bloody acts. Yet women are no strangers to blood; blood is the inhabitant of every woman's house. Women live in the carnage of everyday life: scraped knees, bloody noses, bleeding heads, gory eyes, burning fingers, skinned elbows, stubbed toes, cracked arms, split lips, asthmatic wheezes, burning fever, convulsions, limp bodies, mangled limbs, severed legs, battered skulls. If men study and practice war, women don't have to hunt for slaughter: calamity is their companion.

And women are violent. If not in men's arenas of war, sport, armed disputation, women's violence strikes in more subtle spheres of life. Women's violence is home-made, intimate, an old friend. And so are the objects of woman's violence: child, husband, rival, neighbor, lover; the weapons for this violence are roughly hewn and always close at hand—knife, scissors, breadboard, iron, safety pin, rolling pin, bottle, scalding soup, fire, pepper, poison pot.

In easy reach, as well, is the arsenal of complaint.

> O woman's poor revenge,
> Which dwells but in the tongue.

> —John Webster, "The White Devil," 1612

AND IT IS here that women gain might. Locked in the magic circle of daily life, women become guerrillas of the tongue.

> Sappho, when some fool
> explodes rage
> in your breast,
> hold back that
> yapping tongue!

> —Sappho of Lesbos, Fragment 76

GOSSIPING, nagging, scolding, kvetching, haranguing, lamenting, bellowing, quarreling, squealing, whining, whimpering, cursing, women's voices violate the air. Every whining daughter, bitching sister, nagging wife, scolding mother commits an act of violence.

> So I come to see my son and his family and I wouldn't complain but three hours in her room before she comes down—the kitchen in a mess, the children are hungry, and my son's out getting the barbecue ready—I wouldn't say anything—should I make my son's life worse? A mother is for help—but after all, is she the queen of Sheba?

THE PARTING OF THE WAYS

Bernard Partridge

THE SHRIEKING SISTER.

THE SENSIBLE WOMAN. "*YOU* HELP OUR CAUSE? WHY, YOU'RE ITS WORST ENEMY!"

OFF FOR THE WAR — 1923

"DON'T CRY, DEAR"

cucking stool: noun; bench used mainly for dealing with scolds; i.e., nagging women. The laws of Hereford said that the scold must stand with bare feet and her hair let down so that all could see her.

—John Bellamy, *Crime and Public Order in England...*, 1973

22   How to punish a 'scold'

CHASTITY BELT

In the kitchen, in the bedroom, in the beauty parlor, in the office, on the telephone, women complain.

Dear Susan,

After putting the coffee on, bringing in the paper, I thought, well, I will just sit down and write to dear Susan after finding out from your mother that you mean to sell that beautiful lamp poor Aunt Helen left you. Because it meant so much to her. She always said, "I will never part with it while I'm alive." Well, she's dead and gone now, and her fondest wish was to have that lamp lighting your lovely living room. And now you have betrayed her. And don't think that I couldn't have run down the street and sold that lamp if she had given it to me as she was supposed to. So every time you light the lamp—if you haven't already gotten your money for it—have a laugh and say that old "B–" Aunt Mary may have wanted it but I sure got it. And have fun—life can be pretty dull without a few laughs now and then. But sometime in your life perhaps you should stop and take a good look at yourself—think deeply, why am I rushing, where am I going. Relax, my dear. Enjoy your lovely things. Good luck.

Aunt Mary

AND all women complain, even women who explain that they don't *need* to complain, even those whose job it is to liberate women from having to complain.

I have insisted on using a pseudonym in writing this article because the cost of insisting I am not a cipher would be fatal. If I lost my job, I would have an incredible time finding another. I know I will never "get ahead." Women don't move up through the shelves of a business automatically or by keeping their mouths shut. I could be mocked into an agony of shame for writing this—but beyond that, I could so easily be let go. . . . Listen to me! Think what it is like to have most of your life ahead and be told you are obsolete.

Think what it is like to feel attraction, desire, affection toward others, to want to tell them about yourself, to feel that as-sumption on which self-respect is based, that you are worth something, and that if you like someone, surely he will be pleased to know that . . . I am bitter and frustrated and wasted, but don't you pretend for a minute as you look at me, forty-three, fat, and looking exactly my age, that I am not as alive as you are and that I do not suffer from the category into which you are forcing me.

—Zoe Moss, "It Hurts to Be Alive and Obsolete: The Ageing Woman," *Sisterhood Is Powerful*, edited by Robin Morgan, 1970

YET even with this arsenal of grievance, there are few victories that women win. Their constant battles seldom win empires, sustain territories, or even gain solid ground. Woman's war—her voice nagging, carping, violent—only marks the field of battle. It says: Look at me, see how I suffer, why I suffer, how well I suffer. It rarely says: Look at me, I will not suffer, I will force you not to make me grieve.

For by men we are confounded, though they by us are sometimes crossed. Our tongues are light because earnest in reproving men's filthy vices, and our good counsel is termed nipping injury, in that it accords not with their foolish fancies; our boldness rash, for giving noddies nipping answers, our dispositions naughty, for not agreeing with their vile minds, and our fury dangerous because it will not bear with their knavish behaviors. If our frowns be so terrible and our anger so deadly, men are too foolish in offering occasions of hatred, which shunned, a terrible death is prevented.

—Jane Anger, *Her Protection For Women*, 1589

PART of woman's secret is her covert rage for violence.

I used to lie in bed beside my husband after . . . fights and wish I had the courage to bash in his head with a frying pan. I would do it while he slept, since awake he would overpower me, disarm me. . . . My sexual rage was the most powerful single emotion of my life . . . I would be lying if I said that

St. Radegunde praying

my anger had taught me how to live. But my life has changed because of it. I think I am becoming in many small ways a woman who takes no shit.

—Sally Kempton, "Cutting Loose," *Esquire*, 1970

RADEGUNDE'S WRATH

FOR WOMEN, rage finds constructive release within the communities of women. Sometimes, to their surprise and delight, women find themselves in groups—in families, in churches, in convents, in ballet companies, in unions, in women's colleges, in whorehouses, in encounter groups. They discover that within these groups they have power. Discover that their community has power. And discover that they must tap their talents for violence to maintain their groups. Then women will join together to do battle. These are the wars of women.

The revolt of the nuns at Poitiers, in 589, was fought with imperious and unrelenting passion to maintain control over their nunnery. The convent had been founded in 559 as "a monastery for maidens" by Radegunde, a barbarian princess. Almost immediately, Radegunde was the object of jealousy and hatred, particularly from the Bishop of Poitiers, because of her personal magnetism, learning, and the numbers of women she attracted to her community. This animosity grew over the years as under Radegunde's direction the nunnery at Poitiers developed into a center of power and learning, a place where women could exercise control over their own lives.

The women of the community recognized the great tools of independence Radegunde had given them. At her death in 587 they lamented: "We left our parents, our relatives and our homes, and followed thee. What have we before us now, but tears unceasing, and grief that never can end? Verily, this monastery is to us more than the greatness of village and city . . ."

After Radegunde's death the convent's leadership passed first to her rightful successor, then to an abbess appointed from outside by the Bishop. Remembering the spirit and the teachings of Radegunde, the nuns revolted and prepared for armed hostility. "We are queens," they commanded,

"and we shall not return to the monastery unless the abbess is deposed." Then much blood was shed between the army of the Bishop and the ranks of the nuns.

The armed bands rushed and ran about the monastery by the light of a torch in search of the abbess, and entering the oratory found her extended on the ground in front of the shrine of the Holy Cross. . . . Those who rushed in with bared swords and lances tore her clothes. . . . dragged her away, and placed her in custody near the basilica of St. Hilary. . . . Then in the dark of night they returned to the monastery and not being able to find a light set fire to a barrel. . . . By the light of the bonfire they kindled, they plundered the monastery of all its contents, leaving nothing but what they could not carry off. This happened seven days before Easter.

—Gregory of Tours, sixth century

EVEN nuns openly rebel when the community of women is threatened or abused or violated. Sometimes the community itself becomes a weapon of woman's war. Think of the ballet *Giselle*: the willies—a corps of virgin women pledged to protect their sisters—encircle and defend Giselle, whose heart has just been broken by a young man. She is now taken into the ranks of their sisterhood. So in *Swan Lake*, another army of women fight off the sorcery of love together; theirs is active battle for the freedom of women. So, too, the suffragettes are militant: Emily Knowles throws herself under the hooves of King Edward VI's horse and dies soon after. Edith Pepper remembers a wet, nasty day in 1910: "The government told all the police, 'Knock the women about just as much as you like but don't arrest them.' I should think I was knocked about by a policeman for an hour and I was never thrown onto the floor like some were. Some were very badly injured. It seemed as if there were five or six policemen to stop each weak woman."

And more recently, women's war is announced again in strident terms.

Conspiracy Against Women
WITCH (Women's Independent Taxpayers, Consumers, and Homemakers)

Double, bubble, war and rubble,
When you mess with women, you'll be in trouble.
Who're convicted of murder if abortion is planned.
Convicted of shame if we don't have a man,
Convicted of conspiracy if we fight for our rights,
And burned at the stake when we stand up to fight.
Double, bubble, war and rubble,
When you mess with women, you'll be in trouble.
We curse your empire to make it fall—
When you take on one of us, you take on us all.

—"Witch Document," in *Sisterhood Is Powerful*, 1970

SOMETIMES women consider the constructive use of their united violence. Lysistrata, the leader of the Athenian wives, convinces them that the best way to end the war their husbands are fruitlessly fighting is to deny them sex. The men stop fighting; the women win. Instructing the community of women in their collective potential for power, a writer for the first ladies' magazine in America remembers the enslaved women of Scythia:

We are told that all the women of Scythia once conspired against the men, and kept the secret so well that they executed their design before they were suspected. They surprised them in drink, or asleep; bound them all fast in chains, and having called a solemn council of the whole sex, it was debated what expedient should be used to improve the present advantage, and prevent [the women] falling again into slavery. To kill all the men did not seem to the relish of any of the assembly . . . and they were afterwards pleased to make a great merit of this lenity of theirs. It was therefore agreed to put out the eyes of the whole male sex, and thereby resign for ever after all the vanity they could draw from their [female] beauty in order to secure their authority. "We must no longer pretend to dress and show," said they, "but then we shall be free from servitude; we shall hear no more tender sighs, but, in return, we shall hear no more imperious commands. Love must for ever

Sisterhood as represented in Swan Lake and in a convent.

leave us, but he will carry subjection along with him."

—*Ladies Magazine and Repository*, 1792

WOMEN are violent. This is a well-kept secret, for women themselves are secretive about their violence. Only in the rage of their voices can we scent their intimate kinship with violence. So when the wife nags, she is always silenced by the threat of the cucking stool. And witch or feminist, strident women are, in every century, attacked, persecuted, even tortured beyond their real potential for evil. But sometimes, in groups, women seize hold of their collective right to violence. And then women discover the use of their individual, their secret, powers of violence to publicly honor and acclaim what they desire as women.

SEDUCTION

Coquettes and Consequences

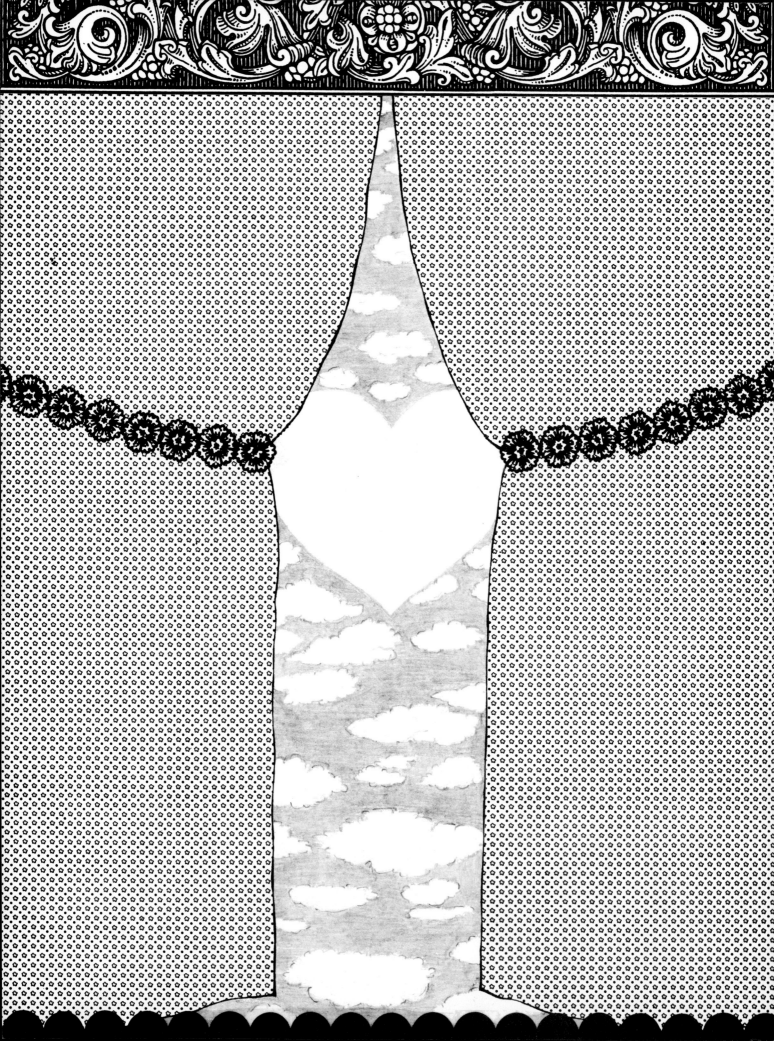

Prologue

WHEN it comes to seduction, the female heart is a theater, and woman a performer in every stage of seduction. She rants and raves and pines and sighs and swoons and swears and swats and, always, delivers lines. Leading lady, understudy, musical comedy queen, prima donna, Scarlett O'Hara, Juliet, Gigi, Carmen, Columbine, Ophelia, Desdemona, Madame Butterfly, Guinivere, Isolde, Brünnhilde, Giselle, Héloïse, Cleopatra, Phèdre, Mimi, Clytemnestra, Circe, Calypso, *La Dame aux Camélias*, Blanche du Bois, Helen of Troy, St. Louis Woman, Irma La Douce, Lolita, Maggie the Cat, soubrette, puppet, comedienne, ingénue, villainess, extra, bit player—she acts. Whatever the guise, she is Coquette; whatever her performance, she, or others, lives its Consequence. And despite the settings, and the scenarios, the lies, the loves, the leers, the tears, it's all the same play. And for every woman there are five acts.

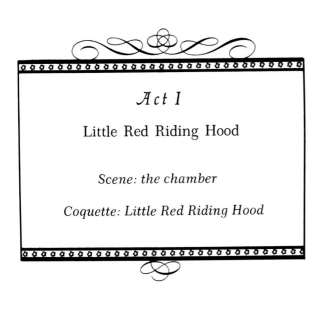

Act I

Little Red Riding Hood

Scene: the chamber

Coquette: Little Red Riding Hood

Action: "Put the cake and the little pot of butter on the bread-bin and get into bed with me."

Little Red Riding Hood undressed and got into bed but she was very surprised to see how her grandmother looked in her night clothes. She said to her:

"What big arms you have, Grandmother!"

"The better to hug you with, my dear!"

"What big legs you have, Grandmother!"

"The better to run with, my child."

"What big ears you have, Grandmother!"

"The better to hear with, my child!"

"What big eyes you have, Grandmother!"

"The better to see you with, my child!"

"What big teeth you have, Grandmother!"

"They're to eat you with!"

So saying, the wicked wolf sprang on
Little Red Riding Hood and ate her up.

—"Little Red Riding Hood,"
The Fairy Tales of Charles Perrault,
translated by Geoffrey Brereton,
seventeenth century

Consequence: Honey, you're very pretty and
you're full of goodies and somebody is
going to eat you up if you're not care-
ful. Now you mustn't cry any more,
men aren't all hairy monsters—forget
what he looked like—someday that
Prince Charming you're always dream-
ing about will come. Until then I guess
the best way of watching out for wolves
is to remember that you belong to yourself and that no one should snatch anything from you until you're willing to
give it up.

Act II

Annie Gets Her Gun

Scene: The bedroom

Coquette: Wench

Action: I'm just a girl who can't say no,
  I'm in a terrible fix.
  I always say come on let's go,
  Just when I ought to say nix.
      "A Girl Who Can't Say No."

I've waited longing for today:
Spindle, bobbin, and spool away.
In joy and bliss I'm off to play
Upon this high holiday.

And when we stop beside the track
At the inn this Sunday, Jack
Will wet my whistle and pay my whack
As on every holiday.

Then he'll take me by the hand
And lay me down upon the land
And make my buttocks feel like sand
Upon this high holiday.

In he'll push and out he'll go,
With me beneath him lying low:
By god's death you do me woe
Upon this high holiday.

Soon my belly begins to swell
As round and great as any bell;
And to my dame I dare not tell
What happened to me this holiday.

Spindle, bobbin, and spool away,
For joy that it's a holiday.

—"The Servant Girl's Holiday,"
late medieval song

Yet she saw, as though her eyes rested on them, his large, strong hands. On the backs of them was a fine golden down that deepened at his wrists. Heavier and darker at the wrists. She found herself praying a little for strength . . . Oh, God, keep my eyes and my thoughts away from him. Away from his hands. Let me keep my eyes and my thoughts away from the golden hairs on his wrists. Let me not think of his wrists. . . .

He . . . began the struggle with the square root of 576. . . . She washed the slate clean with her little sponge. He was leaning close in his effort to comprehend the fiendish little figures that marched so tractably under Selina's masterly pencil. She took it up glibly. . . . "Now, then, suppose you do that for me. We'll wipe it out. There! What must the remainder contain?"

He took it up, slowly, haltingly. The house was terribly still except for the man's voice. . . . A something in his voice—a note—a timbre. She felt herself swaying queerly, as though the whole house were gently rock-

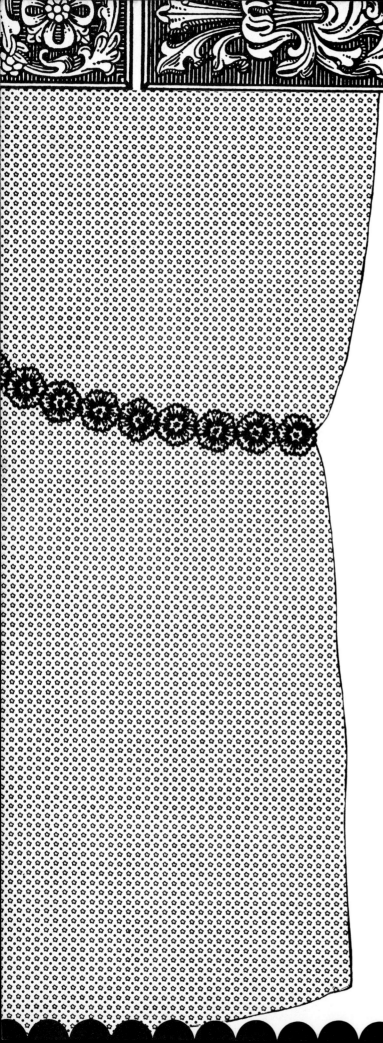

ing. Little delicious agonizing shivers chased each other, hot and cold, up her arms, down her legs, over her spine. . . . Selina's eyes leaped from the book to his hands, uncontrollably . . .

—Edna Ferber, *So Big*, 1924

She . . . went in, pretending to be looking for someone, walking around the bar, then looking at the tables in the back as though she were supposed to find someone she knew. There wasn't anyone of course. Slowly she made her way back past the bar, still looking . . .

"Lookin' for me?"

She smiled before she even saw him because she knew she wouldn't have to go home.

"I don't know," she said. "Who you?"

He was a punk but a cute one. . . .

He finished his own and signaled for two more.

"You better watch out," he said. "Red wine makes me horny as hell."

"Okay," she said, clinking her glass against his. "I'll watch out."

He grinned at her with satisfaction. She was silent, feeling a mixture of emotions from attraction to disdain. How old was he? Maybe not much more than twenty, twenty-two or three at the most. She was too young to be an older woman, surely. She was amused. But beyond all these gentle wine-diluted emotions was amazement at her own distance from them. She could see herself—as though she were both Gulliver and one of the Lilliputians—leaving . . . with this dopey kid, careening home with him, making fun of him, giggling with him, screwing.

—Judith Rossner,
Looking for Mr. Goodbar, 1975

I have a horror of men who know how, I'd rather sleep with a virgin. They take you for an instrument they're proud of knowing how to play. I hate people to bother me, my throat's dry, I'm afraid and I have a bad taste in my mouth and I'm humiliated because they think they dominate me . . .

—Jean-Paul Sartre, *Intimacy*, 1949

Consequence: Sure, it feels good. And it feels good differently with every man. Now that you've run yourself ragged and I have to take care of you, while you're here in bed, think about what you've been doing with your body. A long time ago you would have come crying that you were going to have a baby and you weren't sure who the father was; and when I was young you would have gotten married and hoped that he wouldn't find out that you'd been playing around. Today there are still consequences: you're exhausted from staying up late—I don't care if it *was* in bed; you're not getting anything done that you have to; you don't even have a decent pair of shoes to put on and your apartment's a mess. I'm not saying don't do it. But as long as you're flat on your back alone in bed, try to learn something about yourself and what's been going on. You've been living in a sensual stupor—I mean sex is a drug—it's magic but you can get dopey on it. The important thing to learn is what having lots of sex means about you. How you like to feel, how you can make men feel, what you can do, that you're not a pawn or a sucker; that you don't have to take the first man—you can take the second or the third; or the second *and* the third, and the fifteenth, too. What you're doing is flexing your muscles—and not just the muscles between your legs. Anyway, have some more soup.

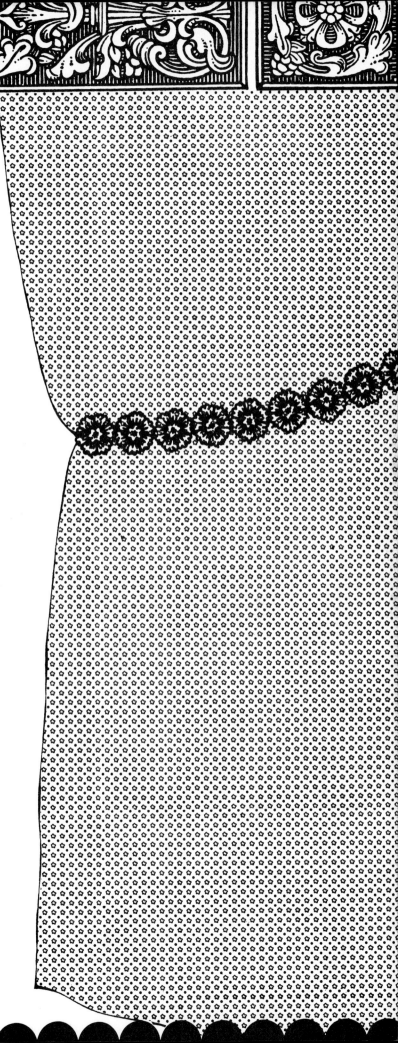

Act III

Blues for Dido

Scene: the kitchen

Coquette: Wailing Woman

Action:　In Tarrytown,
　　　　　There did dwell,
　　　　　A lovely youth,
　　　　　I loved him well,
　　　　　He courted me,
　　　　　My life away,
　　　　　But with me
　　　　　He will no longer stay.

　　　　　Wide and deep,
　　　　　My grave will be,
　　　　　With the wildgoose grasses
　　　　　Growing over me . . .

　　　　　　　—"Tarrytown," American ballad

Cleopatra: No more but e'en a woman, and
　　　commanded
　　　By such poor passion as the maid that
　　　milks
　　　And does the meanest chores. It were for
　　　me
　　　To throw my sceptre at the injurious gods,
　　　To tell them that this world did equal
　　　theirs
　　　Till they had stol'n our jewel. All's but
　　　naught.
　　　Patience is sottish, and impatience does
　　　Become a dog that's mad. Then is it sin
　　　To rush into the secret house of death
　　　Ere death dare come to us? How do you,
　　　women? . . .
　　　My noble girls! Ah, women, women, look!
　　　Our lamp is spent, it's out! . . .

Ah, women, women! Come; we have no
friend
But resolution, and the briefest end.

　　　　　　　—Shakespeare,
　　　　　　Antony and Cleopatra, 1607

I should like this to be accepted as my confession. There is no limit to human suffering. When one thinks, "Now I have touched the bottom of the sea—now I can go deeper," it goes deeper. And so it is for ever. I thought last year in Italy: Any shadow more would be death. But this year has been so much more terrible. . . . Suffering is boundless, is eternity. One pain is eternal torment. Physical suffering is—child's play. To have one's breast crushed by a great stone—one could laugh!

　　　　　　—Katherine Mansfield, *Journal,* 1927

Poor Dido was afire, and roamed distraught all over her city; like a doe caught off her guard and pierced by an arrow from some armed shepherd, who from the distance had chased her amid Cretan woods and without knowing it had left in her his winged barb; so that she traverses in her flight forests and mountain tracks on Dicte, with the deadly reed fast in her flesh.

　　　　　　　—Virgil, *The Aeneid*

You can have him,
I don't want him,
He's not worth fighting for.
. . .

He'd be better off with you.
. . .
All I ever wanted to do was
Run my fingers through his curly locks,
Mend his underwear and darn his socks,
. . .
Kiss him gently when he cuddled near,
Give him babies, one for every year.
. . .

Bring the papers
And when they've been read
Spend the balance of the day
in bed
. . .
You can have him
I don't want him
for he's not the man for me . . .

—Irving Berlin, "I Don't Want Him"

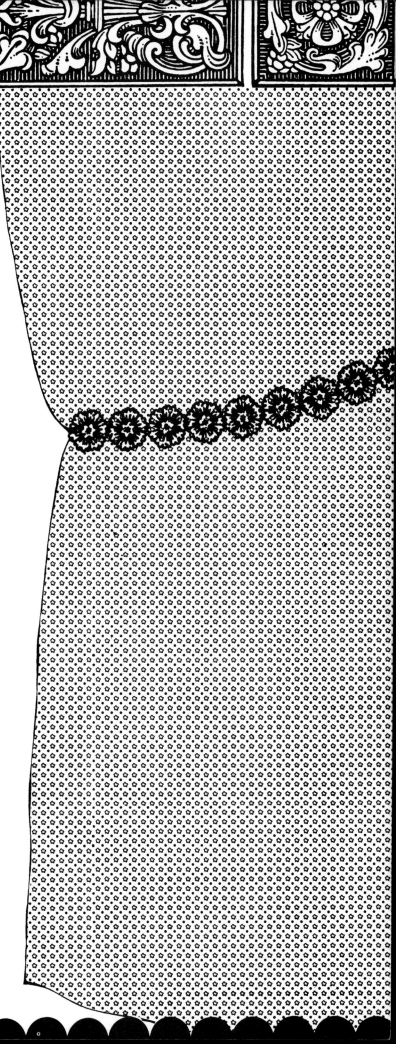

Consequence: You're not going to like what I'm going to say. But I'm going to say it anyway. I know how much he hurt you, the bastard! Don't get mad; if he hurt you, then he's a bastard to me. So what do you think you're going to do now? You can't think? You don't want to think? Oh—you mean you don't want to think because the pain might go away. Okay. But since he went away, let the pain go too. Well, he wasn't any good for you, anyway. And you know what? you weren't any good for him, either. Yeah there were good times. But I mean, you went crazy with love for that man—you weren't even yourself after a while—you gave him your money; you let him use other people's things; you hated anybody he was friendly with—even me. You didn't let him live. So of course he left. And you weren't living, either. I know that you can't think about it. And that you hate men and you don't want any other man. But you've got to find yourself a man. You have to. And get a good one this time. I mean a man who'll give you back to yourself instead of letting you let him steal you away. Know what I mean?

Act IV

Queen Bee

Scene: the honey comb

Coquette: Woman of the world

Action: Get you a young man,
           Raise him to your hand . . .

                                    —Song

Nancy did have a talent. It was for sexual intercourse.

                    —Brigid Brophy, *Flesh*, 1962

Thais: Go away. Do not clutch and tear my garments. It is enough that, in the past, I have yielded to you in sinning . . .

Lovers: Where is she going?

Thais: Where none of you will ever see me.

Lovers: Indeed! What marvel is that that Thais, our delight, who always strove for wealth, who never withdrew her heart from pleasure, who gave herself completely to desire, has now destroyed so much gold and gems and has spurned us, her lovers, with insults and suddenly disappears?

          —Hrotsvitha, *Paphnutius*, tenth century

Why, ay, Alonzo—answered she—'tis true —marriage is indeed for life—but who can tell what sort of a life?—Do you think we can't love without marrying? at least it seems rational to us that have our understanding about us, to try those nearer intimacies, which are said, either to ravish or disgust! to make us fonder or more indifferent. Whatever false notion the world

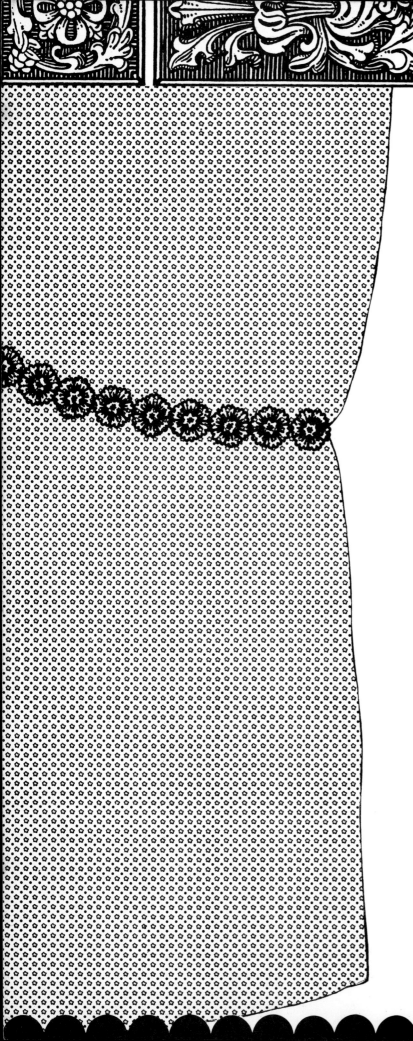

or you may have of virtue, I must confess I should be very loath to bind myself to a man for ever, before I was sure I should like him for a night; I don't take you to be so dull, that I need explain myself any further. I have hinted to you my inclinations, I think it is now your business to convince me of the extent of yours.

> —Mary Manley, *From Secret Memoirs*
> *and Manners of Several Persons*
> of *Quality of Both Sexes*, eighteenth century

I belong to a curious cult
of singing nuns.
We all have padlocked thighs
& knotted knees.
We work the beehive for ink
instead of honey.
& we hum like lovers coming
as we work.

Chastity!
Only the rankest sensualist
gives up sex.

> —Erica Jong, "Chastity," *Loveroot*, 1975

She is mad for the bed of love, but she makes any man she has with her sick.

> —Semonides of Amorgos,
> seventh century B.C.

I, being born a woman and distressed
By all the needs and notions of my kind,
Am urged by your propinquity to find
Your person fair, and feel a certain zest
To bear your body's weight upon my breast:
So subtly is the fume of life designed,
To clarify the pulse and cloud the mind,
And leave me once again undone, possessed.
Think not for this, however, the poor trea-
son
Of my stout blood against my staggering
brain,
I shall remember you with love, or season
My scorn with pity—let me make it plain:
I find this frenzy insufficient reason
For conversation when we meet again.

> —Edna St. Vincent Millay,
> *The Harp-Weaver*, 1920

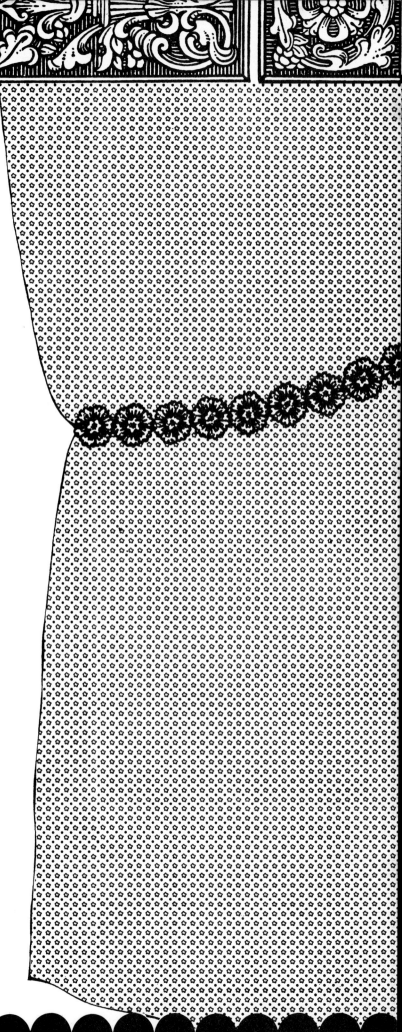

Catherine [the Great]'s need for sexual satisfaction was inexhaustible. When she was
sixty a young lieutenant in the horseguards,
Plato Zubof, by his charm and manner
caught her eye. The machinery was set in
motion. The young man of twenty-five was
examined by the Empress's English physician, Mr. Rogerson, and by Miss Protas,
the royal *éprouveuse*. The latter's function
apparently was to test out the sexual abilities of potential favourites. All was successful and Zubof was duly installed. Not even
England under the Regent had such an office under the crown. . . . The behaviour of
Catherine and her favourites was not an
isolated phenomenon. . . . The majority of
the ladies at court tried to emulate their
sovereign by keeping men as favourites. . . .

—Fernando Henriques,
Prostitution and Society, 1963

Consequence: How the hell do you do it? What
turns out to be honey for you I'd be
scared would be muck for me—I mean,
if I took a man every time I wanted to
I'd be worried about them thinking I
was a black widow spider, merry maybe, but still catching them in snares.
So how do you do it? Don't you worry
that they think you're an old bitch
and that they're just sniffing around
you because you pay them to? I
mean, you do foot the bill, don't you?
I mean how can a young man like that
on his little salary go out to eat or take
those vacations? Sure, some of your
men have been your age, even older,
and some of them have as important
a job as you do, and maybe some of
them even make more money—Oh I
know they're not as good in bed as the
young ones but doesn't that make problems, too? You have to lie to all of
them, anyway—men always ask, has
anybody ever done this to you before,
don't they? So what do you do? And
what happens when you want to be
looked after? I'd be afraid of ending
up a lonely old lady. But you just smile
and lick your lips. More power to you.

Act V

Venus Preserved

Scene: the drawing room

*Coquette: Marie Leveau, voodoo
priestess of New Orleans*

Action: VERA. Oh! Stop that, Natalya Petrovna, leave off, do! . . . Give up speaking to me as though I were a child . . . From to-day I'm a woman . . . I'm as much a woman as you are.

NATALYA PETROVNA (embarrassed). Vera . . .

VERA. . . . He hasn't deceived you. . . . He doesn't care for me, you know that, you've no need to be jealous.

NATALYA PETROVNA. . . . Vera!

VERA. It's the truth . . . don't go on pretending. These pretences are no use now . . . I see through them now, I can assure you. To you I'm not the ward you are watching over (Ironically) like an elder sister. . . . (Moves closer to her.) I'm your rival.

—Ivan Turgenev,
A Month in the Country, 1850

Now, however, she was thinking about her son. Every mother has to endure it, I suppose, she thought. The marvellous intimacy could not last. . . . He had become untouchable; and Harriet, with her long habit of touching, was suddenly in a dilemma, in an anguish. She was visited by alarmingly precise ghostly yearnings. Feeling very like the torments of an unrequited love made her blush and tremble. . . . She wanted to hold him in her arms again, to cover him with kisses, to untangle with caressing fingers that untidy and now absurdly long golden hair. . . . She knew of mothers who flirted with their adolescent sons.

—Iris Murdoch, *The Sacred and Profane Love Machine*, 1975

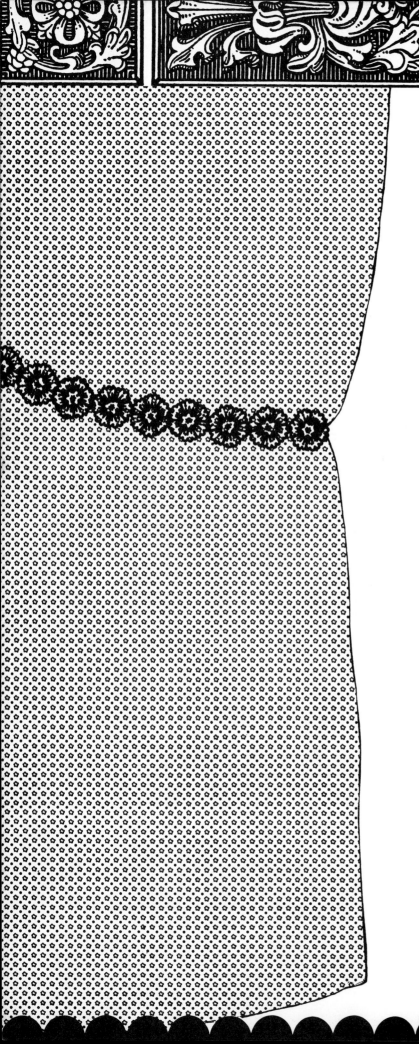

Laurence examined her mother in the mirror. The perfect, the ideal picture of a woman who is ageing well. Who is ageing. It was a picture Dominique would not accept. For the first time she was showing weakness—flinching. Hitherto she had taken the lot, illnesses, hard knocks, everything. And now suddenly there was panic in her eyes.

'I can't believe that one day I'll be seventy.'

'There's no woman who stands up to it as well as you do,' said Laurence.

'My body's all right; I don't envy anyone. But look here.' She pointed to her eyes, and her neck. Obviously, she was no longer in her forties.

'You aren't in your twenties any more, obviously,' said Laurence.

'But lots of men prefer women who know their way about. Take Gilbert . . . Gilbert . . . It's to keep him that I destroy myself going out all the time. The danger is that it may turn against me.'

'Oh, come now!'

Dominique put on her Balenciaga suit. Never anything from Chanel: you spend a fortune to look as if you dressed at a second-hand stall. 'That cow Marie-Claire,' she murmured. 'She obstinately refuses to divorce: just for the pleasure of bitching me.'

'Perhaps she'll give way in the end.'

There was no sort of doubt that Marie-Claire said 'that cow Dominique.' In the days of Lucile de Saint-Chamont Gilbert still lived with his wife: the question did not even arise, since Lucile had children and a husband. Dominique had made him leave Marie-Claire: if he had yielded it was because it suited him, fair enough; but even so Laurence had thought her mother pretty savage.

—Simone de Beauvoir,
Les Belles Images, 1966

Teasers grin but don't bear it, they want to attract men and bask in their admiration, but not reap the consequences. They will not sin for their supper.

Prickteasers flirt and tease, chatter and

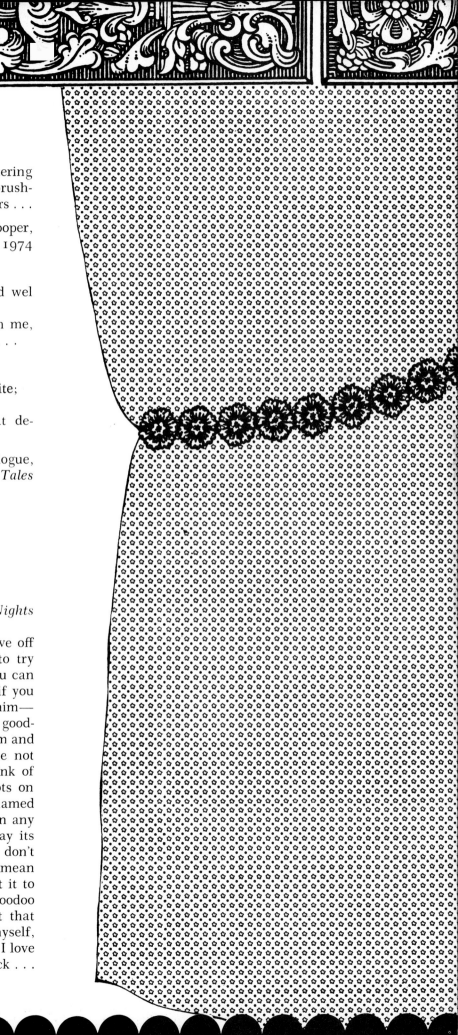

giggle, produce a force-ten gale fluttering their false eye-lashes, and are always brushing imaginary crumbs off men's trousers . . .

—Jilly Cooper,
Women and Super Women, 1974

As help me God, I was a lusty one
And faire, and riche, and yonge, and wel
  begone:
And trewely, as min husbondes tolden me,
I had the best queint that mighte be. . . .
I loved never by no discretion,
But every folwed min owne appetite,
All were he shorte, longe, blake or white;
I toke no kepe, so that he liked me,
How poure he was, ne eke of what de-
  gree. . . .

—Chaucer, Wife of Bath's Prologue,
The Canterbury Tales

I used to dye my hair
But time undyed it.
Now I am sage,
I show my bottom bare
Which does not age.
(I used to hide it.)

—"White Hair," *Arabian Nights*

Consequence: Listen, you old witch, leave off him. He's mine and I'm going to try to keep him. I know very well you can get him if you want him—even if you are an old hag. You don't need him— you don't want him. Sure, you're a good- looking woman—you've got charm and a wicked tongue and you're sure not shy. But your neck is lined—think of your age! You've got old-age spots on the backs of your hands. I'd be ashamed of putting hands as old as that on any man's body. It's horrible—you say its only sex in the head for you. I don't understand that—what do you mean by talking sexy if you don't want it to end up in bed? You're doing a voodoo trick on him, and I haven't got that kind of witchery. I've just got myself, and a good, young body. Besides, I love him—please let me have him back . . .

Epilogue

LADY WISHFORT: . . . In what figure shall I give his heart the first impression? There is a great deal in the first impression. Shall I sit?—No, I won't sit—I'll walk—ay, I'll walk from the door upon his entrance; and then turn full upon him.—No, that will be too sudden. I'll lie—ay, I'll lie down—I'll receive him in my little dressing-room; there's a couch—yes, yes, I'll give the first impression on a couch.—I won't lie neither, but loll and lean upon one elbow, with one foot a little dangling off, jogging in a thoughtful way—yes—yes—and then as soon as he appears, start, ay, start and be surprised and rise to meet him in a pretty disorder—yes—oh, nothing is more alluring than a levee from a couch in some confusion. It shows the foot to advantage, and furnishes with blushes, and recomposing airs beyond comparison. Hark! There's a coach.

—Congreve, *The Way of the World*, 1700

Eye, Hand and Mind

Neither arrogance nor presumption drives us to the audacity of wanting to be like God—that is, like man; we are not like Eve of old.

—Emma Jung, *Animus and Anima,* 1957

EVE from Adam's rib, the goddess Athene out of her father Zeus' head: while women give biological birth, men—at least in legend—give women's minds life. And not just in legend: through time, women's access to knowledge has come mostly through men. Learned lady after learned lady speaks of a father or brother or husband or lover or son who, coming back to the waiting women at home, shares the exhilaration of the waves of thought outside.

Men stand, as it were, upon a promontory, commanding extensive views, and open to immediate impulses from all above, below, and around them. Women sit like genii of secluded caves, receiving echoes, and communicating mere reverberations from the outer world.

—Jane Williams, *The Literary Women of England*, 1861

While I was still very small, [my father] won me over by his gaiety and gift of gab; as I grew older I came to admire him for more serious reasons: I was amazed at his culture, his intelligence, and his infallible good sense. . . . It was he who had introduced my mother to life and the world of books. . . . As I grew up, he paid more and more attention to my education. . . . In particular he took great pains with my handwriting and spelling: whenever I wrote him a letter, he would send it back to me, with corrections. . . . In order to help form my taste in literature, he had assembled a little anthology for me in an exercise book covered with shiny black imitation leather. . . . He never intimidated me, in the sense that I never felt the slightest uneasiness in his presence; but I did not attempt to bridge the distance that lay between us; there were many subjects that I could not imagine myself discussing with him; to him I was neither body nor soul, but simply a mind. Our relationship was situated in a pure and limpid atmosphere where unpleasantness could not exist. He did not condescend to me, but raised me up to his level, and then I was proud to feel myself a grown-up person.

—Simon de Beauvoir, *Memoirs of a Dutiful Daughter*, 1958

I am far from wishing to place any obstacles in the way of the intellectual advancement and development of women. On the contrary, I don't see how we are to make any permanent advancement while one-half of the race is sunk, as nine-tenths of women are, in mere ignorant parsonese superstitions; and to show you that my ideas are practical I have fully made up my mind, if I can carry out my plans, to give my daughters the same training in physical science as their brother will get. . . . They, at any rate, shall not be got up as man-traps for the matrimonial market. If other people would do the like the next generation would see women fit to be the companions of men in all their pursuits—though I don't think that men have anything to fear from their competition.

—Thomas Huxley, *Life and Letters*, 1901

EVEN when men have been less than generous, some women struggled to create themselves out of the books of men.

By the time I was four years old I read English perfectly, and having a great memory, I was carried to sermons. . . . When I was about seven years of age, I remember I had at one time eight tutors in several qualities, languages, music, dancing, writing, and needle-work; but my genius was quite averse from all but my book, and that I was so eager of, that my mother, thinking it prejudiced my health, would moderate me in it; yet this rather animated me than kept me back, and every moment I could steal from my play I would employ in any book I could find, when my own were locked up from me.

—Lucy Hutchinson, *Autobiography*,
seventeenth century

Dear Miss Dow—
. . . I will give you now a rough list of authors and books, the principal ones; without attempt at classification:
Authors with whom I am very well acquainted:—Shakespeare, Dickens, Eliot, Scott, Tennyson, Milton, Wordsworth . . .
Well acquainted with:
—Hawthorne, Browning, Kipling, Barrie, Mark Twain . . .

Slightly acquainted with:
—Bacon, Addison, Lamb . . .
Have read:
—Tolstoi, Ann Karenina; Kingsley, Hypathia; Holmes, Elsie Venner, and Autocrat of the Breakfast Table . . .
This list must seem awfully crazy to you. I've really read so much that I hardly know what to pick out.

> Very sincerely,
> Vincent Millay [October 23, 1912; age 20]

. . . tentatively, reluctantly, I'm becoming interested in no less than my infant room. From the reading I do in the early hours before the household wakes, how could I not become interested? Freud, Adler, Lipmann, Scheiner, Jung and Bertrand Russell explaining life and children, and all the poetry at night. I am my own university, I my own Professor.

—Sylvia Ashton-Warner, *Myself*, 1941

SOLITARY self-education is a fact of women's lives.

[Queen Elizabeth's] mind, said [Ascham] seemed to be free from female weakness, and her power of application was like a man's. . . . They began the day by reading the New Testament in Greek, and then passages from Sophocles, which Ascham had chosen not only for their beauty but because they contained ideas which he thought would strengthen her mind against misfortune. She spent hours translating works from one foregin language into another and conversing with Ascham on intellectual topics in all the languages in turn; her favorite study, however, was history. She liked to spend three hours a day reading it, and would study the same period in all the different books she could get hold of. Her handwriting was now of exquisite beauty. Her manners, too, charmed him, they were so gracious and so modest. Another trait that aroused his admiration was the plainness of her dress and hair. "She greatly prefers a simple elegance to show and splendour," he wrote, "despising the outward adorning of plaiting the hair and wearing of gold."

—Elizabeth Jenkins,
Elizabeth the Great, 1958

AND decided to act. Sappho, for instance, the notorious poet from the island of Lesbos, took really subversive action. She loved the young girls in the school she founded but she educated them, too. "I taught the talented/and furthermore, I did/well in instructing/Hero, who was a girl/track star from Gyara." For her efforts Sappho gained fame as the tenth Muse of poetry, and eternal damnation as well as the seductress of maidens' minds and bodies. People often fear that learning and the pursuit of education by women for women is an aggressive, unsexing act. In the Greece of Sappho's day, most good women just stayed home. But

just as a mongrel dog is allowed more freedom to go abroad than is accorded to a thoroughbred, so there are women in ancient Athens who were not the victims of such an incarceration as befell the citizen matron; these were for the most part foreign women, who were often intelligent and educated. Their life was very different; they were free and at the same time respected; at least it was respectable to associate with them. They were the famous Hetairae. . . . [Aspasia] was the mistress of Pericles, and Plato says that she even composed the famous Funeral Oration. . . . It is of great significance to the history of women to note this example of a division of labour and of morality, of a dual standard between women in one society . . .

—John Langdon-Davies,
A Short History of Women, 1928

So, TOO, with the women of the Middle Ages in Western Europe. Education in religious houses offered women released time from the drudgery and stillness of daily life.

The monotony of life in the castles or burghs of this period can hardly be exaggerated. . . . The young nobleman followed his father to camp and court, where he tasted of the experiences of life; the young noblewoman stayed at home, cut off from intercourse with those of her age and standing, and from every possibility of widening her mental horizon.

—Lina Eckenstein,
Woman Under Monasticism, 1896

THEIR men off fighting, the women clustered together like concubines in the harem of a heathen Saracen. But Frankish princesses or, later, Victorian gentlewomen, the daughters of Eve have always been quick to seize any escape route to the world outside—even when, as in the Middle Ages, they exchanged one cloister (the manor house) for another cloister (the convent).

. . . the religious settlement was an endowed college where girls were received to be trained, and where women who wished to devote themselves to learning and the arts permanently resided.

—*Woman Under Monasticism*

AND devote themselves they did. Gradually, through strenuous effort, women became learned and powerful in and out of the convent. At the helm of great feudal households and prosperous abbeys, they exercised political clout and at the same time cultivated small gardens in the midst of barbaric life. In France the great chateaux ceased to be simply the knight's defensive post. Its mistress, the *midon*, transformed barracks and battlements into the court, a seat of learning and culture. Christine de Pisan, in the fifteenth century, was the first historian of France and the first secular poet. But this "man of letters," France's first, was a woman, a twenty-five-year-old widow with three small children to support. Like all women of her time, officialdom considered her uneducated. Why? Because learning, which meant Latin and Greek, was the province of men, particularly clergymen under whose aegis men only were trained. So, like Sappho, Christine de Pisan wrote of what women were permitted to know: accounts of the time, politics, the poetry of personal experience—sexual love, marriage, widowhood, and, interestingly, the condition of women.

A girl of sixteen (isn't it an unnatural thing?) who doesn't find her armor heavy; it seems that her upbringing is responsible for that, she is so strong and hardy; And before her flees the enemy, no one stands up to her. She has done it, many eyes watching, and with them goes France clearing away ruins as she wins back her castles and cities . . . Didn't she lead the king whom she held by the hand to his coronation?

—Christine de Pisan,
"On Joan of Arc," 1429

So OUT of Eden, woman tends a garden lush with flowers and weeds and fruits of her own imaginings. It is she, in fact, who domesticates thought, wrenching it from the dominion of the church and the law. And as Adam followed Eve through the tangles of that other garden and also bit the apple, so men assemble around the *midon* and under her patronage create the literature of daily love and domestic life. The troubadors, men and women, start to sing.

All other joys bow down to it,
And all other riches obey
Milord—for her beautiful bearing
And her beautiful, charming looks.
A man would have to be more than a hundred
Who could seize the joy of her love. . . .

—Duke William IX of Aquitaine,
twelfth century

Now I must sing of what I have no will,
For greatly am I tried by him I love,
The one I love above all things;
He sees no worth in mercy or in manners;
My beauty's nothing, like my conduct and
   my sense,
For he deceives and cheats me as if I
Were nothing more than just a homely
   wretch. . . .

My merit should help me, my lineage too,
My beauty, and even more, my loyal heart;
And so I'm sending over to your abode
This little song to serve as my messenger;
And please reply, my sweet and handsome
   lover,
Why you're so harsh, so very cruel to me.
Tell me: is it arrogance or wicked will?

> The Countess of Dia, "The wife
> of Lord William of Peiteius, a
> beautiful and good woman. And
> she fell in love with Lord Raim-
> baut of Orange and wrote of him
> many good songs."

—twelfth century

AND while the troubadours sing the clerics
shout: Woman is wicked.

Of the numberless snares that the crafty
enemy spreads for us over all the hills and
fields of the world, the worst, and the one
which scarcely anyone can avoid, is woman,
sad stem, evil root, vicious fount, which in
all the world propagates many scandals.
Woman, sweet evil, honey and poison alike,
anointing with balm the sword with which
thou piercest even wise men's hearts. Who
persuaded our first parent to taste the forbidden thing? A woman. Who forced the
father to defile his daughters? A woman.
Who tamed the strong by robbing him of
his hair? A woman. Who cut off the sacred
head of a just man with a sword? A
woman . . .

—Marbode, Bishop of Rennes,
eleventh century

THOUGH plagued by the appetites of the beasts,
man shares with the angels their powers of
reason. He can understand the word of God,
woman cannot. Lesser being, born of Adam's
rib, God's afterthought, she cannot think. She
does not deserve the written word.

To you, learned men, who abide in wisdom
and are unenvious of another's progress,
and well-disposed towards him as befits the
truly learned, I, Hrotsvith, though I am un-
learned and lacking in thoroughness, ad-
dress myself. . . .
   I cannot sufficiently thank you for the
help of your liberal generosity and for your
kindness towards me; you, who have been
trained in the study of philosophy and
have perfected yourselves in the pursuit of
knowledge, have held my writings, those
of a lowly woman, worthy of admiration,
and have praised with brotherly affection
the power which works in me. You have
declared that there is in me a certain knowledge of that learning the essence of which
is beyond my woman's understanding. . . .
I am divinely gifted with abilities. . . . Lest
this gift of God in me should be wasted
through neglect, I have sought to pluck
threads and pieces from the garments of
philosophy, and have introduced them into
my . . . work so that my own moderate
knowledge may be enhanced by the addition
of their greater worth, and God, who grants
power, may be praised by so much the more
as a woman's power is held to be inferior.

—The Nun Hrotsvith,
poet-dramatist-historian, tenth century

IT IS at great cost over the next seven hundred
years that woman turn to the books of men.

Taught to read at home, [Elizabeth Hamil-
ton] soon found in books "a substitute even
for a playmate." She attended a boarding
school for some time and after leaving it
continued to educate herself. Her relatives
were somewhat alarmed by her precocity.
On one occasion, finding a copy of Lord
Kame's *Elements of Criticism* under the
cushion of a chair, Mrs. Marshall reproved
her niece "lest she should be detected in a
study which prejudice and ignorance might
pronounce unfeminine."

—Introduction, by Gina Luria,
to *Memoirs of Modern Philosophers*
(originally published in 1800),
by Elizabeth Hamilton

The education of the English boy . . . was considered a much more serious matter than the education of the English boy's sister. My parents, especially my father, discussed the question of my brother's education as a matter of real importance. My education and that of my sister were scarcely discussed at all. Of course we went to a carefully selected girls' school, but beyond the facts that the head mistress was a gentlewoman and that all the pupils were girls of my own class, nobody seemed concerned.

—Emmeline Pankhurst,
My Own Story, 1914

Long before an American girl arrives at the marriageable age, her emancipation from maternal control begins: she has scarcely ceased to be a child when she already learns things for herself, and acts on her own impulses. . . . An American girl scarcely ever displays that virginal softness in the midst of young desires or that innocent and in-

genuous grace which usually attends the European woman in the transition from girlhood to youth. It is rare that an American woman, at any age, displays childish timidity or ignorance. Like the young women of Europe she seeks to please, but she knows precisely the cost of pleasing. If she does not abandon herself to evil, at least she knows that it exists; and she is remarkable rather for purity of manners than for chastity of mind.

—Alexis de Tocqueville,
Democracy in America, 1835

Mrs. Macaulay is better employed reddening her cheeks than blackening a man's character.

—Samuel Johnson, on Catherine Macaulay,
eighteenth-century historian

Cornelia, had she not been a woman, would have deserved the first place among philosophers.

—Cicero, on the Roman matron
and lecturer Cornelia

I have realized in my inmost soul that most subtle outlawry of the feminine intellect, which warns it off from the highest fields of research.

—Antoinette Brown Blackwell,
Sexes Throughout Nature, 1875

I know of no way of rendering classical knowledge so ridiculous as by clothing it in petticoats . . . more amicable accomplishments than reading Greek are attainable by a female mind . . . because a few have gained applause by studying the dead languages, all womankind should assume their Dictionaries and Lexicons; else we might soon expect to see Westminster School a female Academy, or (as the ladies make rapid advances towards *manhood*) we might in a few years behold a sweepstakes rode by women . . .

—"On Female Authorship"
Ladies Magazine, January 1793

BUT, clearly, women are often willing to incur the necessary expense. And sometimes, in particular historical eras, they did so in great numbers, as in the Renaissance when women learned and made active use of their knowledge.

> Little girls should learn Latin: it completes their charms.
>
> —Cardinal Bembo, sixteenth century

In Renaissance Italy, for instance,

> intellectual attainments were not only counted appropriate for women, but they were recognized as a distinct added attraction. Every city of importance had women whose renown was a source of civic pride. Women not only studied under tutors, but they apparently attended classes in the great universities and even occupied important chairs in the most distinguished faculties.
>
> —Myra Reynolds, *The Learned Lady*, 1922

And of Renaissance England we are told,

> There are no Accounts in History of so many truly great Women in any one age, as are to be found between the years 1500–1600.
>
> —William Wotton, seventeenth century

Women participated effectively in the life of their times in Renaissance England, France, Germany, Italy. They financed many of the great achievements of the epoch: Shake-

speare's plays; Raleigh's voyages; Columbus's discoveries. Queen Elizabeth nurtured religious tolerance and oversaw the great Elizabethan Compromise; ladies undertook the establishment of private "colleges" where young men practiced the new arts of Chymestrie, Physics, the Inductive process of Rational Enquiry, and architecture.

In England, this era of intellectual expansion began with the arrival of Catherine of Aragon, first wife of Henry VIII, at the English court. Educated "like a man" herself while a young woman at the Spanish court, Catherine brought notable European scholars to England to educate her daughter, who became the infamous "Bloody Mary." Learned treatises which appeared during Catherine's reign, 1523–38, supported women's claims to enlightenment, yet none was written by a woman. The emphases in these tracts rested on woman's place in the home: "housewifery," spinning, cooking, the use of medicinal herbs, and the moral efficacy of learning. All these tracts agreed, however, that women were not public creatures; therefore, occupations which involved publicity (like writing and teaching) were not suitable for women.

Althoug Queen Elizabeth I was the classic Learned Lady of this era, she was by no means alone: Anne Killigrew, mother and teacher of Francis Bacon, the philosopher; Lady Jane Grey, a scholarly recluse martyred for the political ambitions of her husband and father; Mary Sidney, translator with her brother, Sir Philip Sidney, of the Book of Psalms and herself an experimental chemist who supported men chemists at her home, Wilton House. Margaret, favorite daughter of Sir Thomas More, was educated by her father in the same manner as his sons. She became famous throughout Europe for her erudition—languages, philosophy, theology. Yet she was praised by her father and contemporaries "because she studies for love of learning, not for fame, and contents herself with her husband and father as a sufficient audience." She directed her learning to the education of her five children and had Greek and Latin tutors for her daughters as well as for her sons.

Despite their restriction to the private sphere, women in this period were admitted to the learning and intellectual advancements which are the privilege of the well-connected and the wealthy. For nearly fifty years learned men made easy space for learned ladies.

But woman's performance during the Renaissance did not silence her critics. Even those men who fought for the rights of women to be educated insisted that woman's first place was in the home.

> Neither is there anie difference in harvest time, whether it was man or woman, that sowed first the corne: for both of them beare name of a reasonable creature equally, whose nature reason only doth distinguish from bruite beastes, and therfore I do not see shy learning in like manner may not eequally agree with both sexes; for by it, reason is cultivated, and (as a fielde) sowed with wholesome precepts, it bringeth excellent fruit. But if the soyle of woman's braine be of its own nature bad, and apter to bear fearne than corne (by which saying manie doe terrifye women from learning) I am of opinion therefore that a woman's witt is the more diligently by good instructions and learning to be manured, to the ende, the defect of nature may be redressed by industrie.
>
> —Thomas More, letter, sixteenth century

OTHER, more important men took a harsher stand. Martin Luther remarked, "Women should remain at home, sit still, keep house and bear and bring up children." And then again: "If woman grows weary and at last dies from childbearing, it matters not. Let her only die from bearing. She is there to do it." Under Luther's leadership, the Reformation marked the beginning of social individualism for men. It also marked the end of systematic education for women.

> In the convents the female portion of the population found their only teachers, the rich as well as the poor, and the destruction of these religious houses . . . was the absolute extinction of any systematic education for women during a long period.
>
> —Gasquet, *Henry VIII and the English Monasteries*, 1889

So? WHY does education matter, anyway? And what is it? Why does anyone struggle for it?

Consider what it's like to live uneducated.

Try to follow the maps of any underground subway system; there are no visual landmarks and you have to be able to read the signs. You can get fifty people to direct you and still stay lost.

Then think of writing and arithmetic. How do you make a grocery list for a holiday dinner without being able to determine quantities, amounts, roasting time per pound—or without being able to spell asparagus, yoghurt, maraschino cherry, or banana? And when a child's sick with a fever, think of reading the thermometer, or copying down the doctor's instructions—the pink medicine four times a day, the orange every three hours, two aspirin every four hours until the fever is under 101— and a tepid bath the minute the fever rises above 102.

It's very hard to be uneducated.

If Mrs. Santana knew as much about home economics as the people who draw up welfare budgets, and if she shopped judiciously once a week at the supermarket across the street . . . she could spend far less. Instead, she frequents a *bodega* a few doors away from the supermarket, and with good reason: when she runs out of money between welfare checks, as she inevitably does, the *bodega* will give her credit and the supermarket won't. There are no giant economy sizes, no specials, no money-saving house brands at the *bodega*, where prices of most items are about twenty percent higher than at the supermarket, but it has not been Mrs. Santana's experience that saving a few

dollars on groceries has appreciably affected her situation . . .

If [Mrs. Santana's] children come home for lunch because they don't like the free meal the school is serving and she runs out of something, she sends them across the street to charge another loaf of bread, another quart of milk. After lunch, she buys whatever she thinks she will need for dinner. The children are constantly in and out of the *bodega* during the afternoon and evening . . . charging snacks . . . or replacements for whatever the household has just run out of: two rolls of toilet paper, a small bottle of cooking oil, a box of soap powder.

—Susan Sheehan, "A Welfare Mother,"
The New Yorker, September 29, 1975

Domestic mismanagement during illness is another not uncommon cause of death in infancy. Many mothers are continuously administering medicines of one kind or another and thereby derange instead of promoting the healthy operation of the infant system. Such persons never stop for a moment to inquire what the *cause* is, whether it has been or can be removed, or whether its removal will not of itself be sufficient to restore health . . . we have no hesitation in expressing our conviction that a child can encounter few greater dangers than that of being subjected to the vigorous discipline of a medicine-giving mother . . .

—Edward John Tilt, M.D.,
*The Elements of Health and Principles
of Female Hygiene*, London, 1852

The freedom of her people depended upon their ability to read the "No trespassing" signs, therefore, she clandestinely acquired the fundamental reading skills and passed them on to her followers. "We went every day [to school] with our books wrapped in paper to prevent the police or white person from seeing them."

—Susie King Taylor, *Reminiscences of
My Life in Camp with the 33 Colored
Troops*, Boston, 1962

EDUCATION can improve health and welfare and even sometimes promote happiness.

Lady Journalist: Do women want to be educated more than men?
Response: Yes.
Lady Journalist: Why?

WOMEN always live in the welter of woman's wisdom—which is not always wise, or even smart. The greatest service which women can give to themselves or each other is to emancipate woman's mind from the conditions of woman's life. So for women the tools of freedom and the emblems of it are education.

Before having a child I was always trying to give my students purely intellectual information. Now I realize that there must be a continuity between public and private life. The abstract thinking that one learns in a university can and should be applied to the way one lives one's life.

—Helen McNeil, "The New Bluestockings,"
Queen Magazine, 1975

SAPPHO recognized this, Hrotsvith recognized it; so did Christine de Pisan, so did Mary Astell. A daughter of her time, she taught herself the ABC's of the bitter religious controversies which erupted into civil war in England. One of the many women of the seventeenth century, anonymous and named, who transformed doctrinal dispute into feminist polemic, Astell's first concern was education for women. In the controversial *A Serious Proposal for the Ladies* (1690) she suggested the foundation of a house of "Religious Retirement for gentlewomen where devotion to learning and religion would replace the frivolity and emptiness of their lives." If this sounds familiar, remember Sappho and the medieval convents. Yet the convents were dissolved, and likewise Astell's school never got off the ground. So with bitterness in a later tract, *Reflections on Marriage*, she pointed her finger to the evils which always follow when women are squatters.

In the first place, Boys have much Time and Pains, Care and Cost bestowed on their education, Girls have little or none. [Boys] are early initiated in the Sciences, are made acquainted with Antient and Modern Discoveries, they Study Books and Men, have all imaginable encouragement; not only Fame . . . But also Title, Authority, Power, and Riches themselves which purchase all these things, are the reward of their im-

provement. [Girls] are restricted, frown'd upon, beat, not *for* but *from* the Muses; Laughter and Ridicule that never-failing Scare-Crow is set up to drive them from the Tree of Knowledge. But if in spite of all these difficulties Nature prevails, and they can't be kept so ignorant as their masters would have them, they are stared upon as Monsters, Censur'd, Envy'd and ever discouraged, or at the best they have the Fate the Proverb assigns them: *Virtue is praised and starved.*

—Astell, *Reflections on Marriage,* 1700

WOMEN have always sharpened their minds on the gristle and bone of their century's religion: Feudalism, Catholicism, Humanism, Protestantism, Fraternalism, Industrialism, Darwinism, Marxism, Freudianism, Communism, Fascism, Sexism. Inevitably their teeth grow strong. Those who feed on ideas to become learned—like Astell in the seventeenth century, or Mary Wollstonecraft in the eighteenth century, or Margaret Fuller and Elizabeth Cady Stanton in the nineteenth century, Simone de Beauvoir and Margaret Sanger in the twentieth century—come to expect substantial fare, steak instead of spun-sugar confections. A little learning *is* a dangerous thing —yet once out of the kitchen en route to the classroom or the typewriter or the stage or the street or the pulpit, woman feels the pangs of a new kind of hunger.

The twenty years between 1815 and 1835 see . . . the first indications of independent trade union action among women [factory] workers. . . . But there is a paradox of feeling even in this advance. The Radicalism of northern working women was compounded of nostalgia for lost status and the assertion of new-found rights. According to conventions which were deeply felt, the woman's status turned upon her success as a housewife in the family economy, in domestic management and forethought, baking and brewing, cleanliness and child-care. The new independence, in the mill or full-time at the loom, which made new claims possible, was felt simultaneously as a loss in status and in personal independence. . . . [Women] looked back to a "golden" past in which home earnings . . . could be gained around their own door. . . . In good times

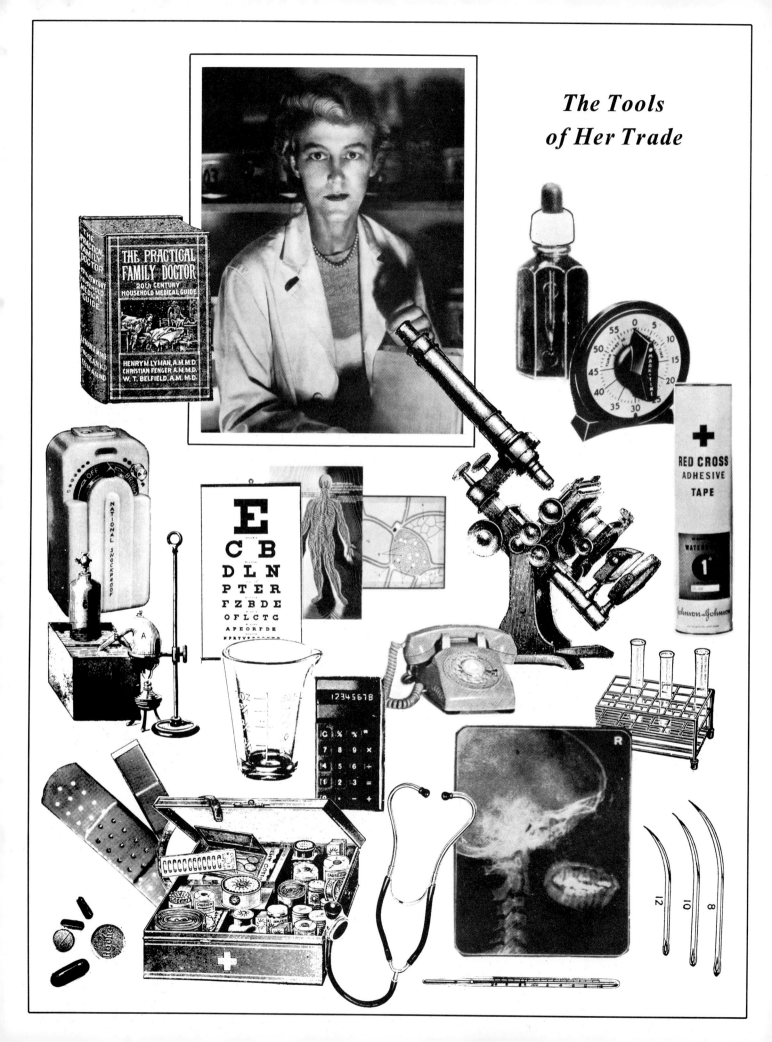

The Tools
of Her Trade

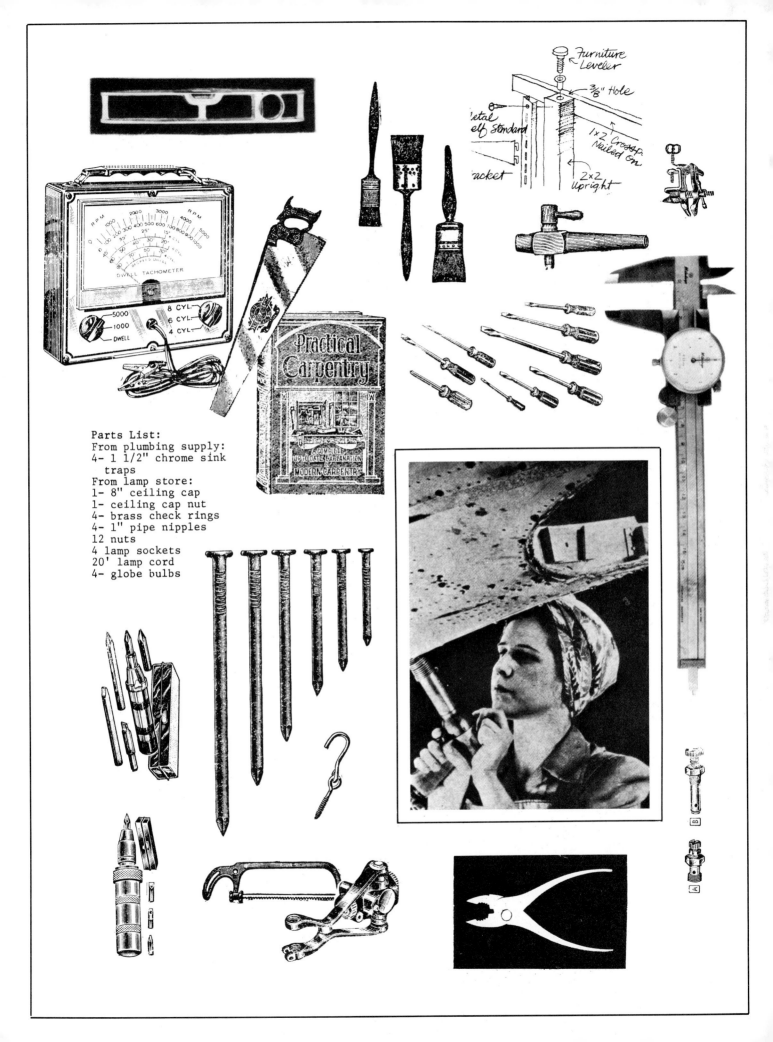

Furniture Leveler
3/8" Hole
Metal Shelf Standard
Bracket
1x2 Crosspc. Nailed On
2x2 Upright

Practical Carpentry
A COMPLETE UP-TO-DATE EXPLANATION OF MODERN CARPENTRY

Parts List:
From plumbing supply:
4- 1 1/2" chrome sink
   traps
From lamp store:
1- 8" ceiling cap
1- ceiling cap nut
4- brass check rings
4- 1" pipe nipples
12 nuts
4 lamp sockets
20' lamp cord
4- globe bulbs

B

A

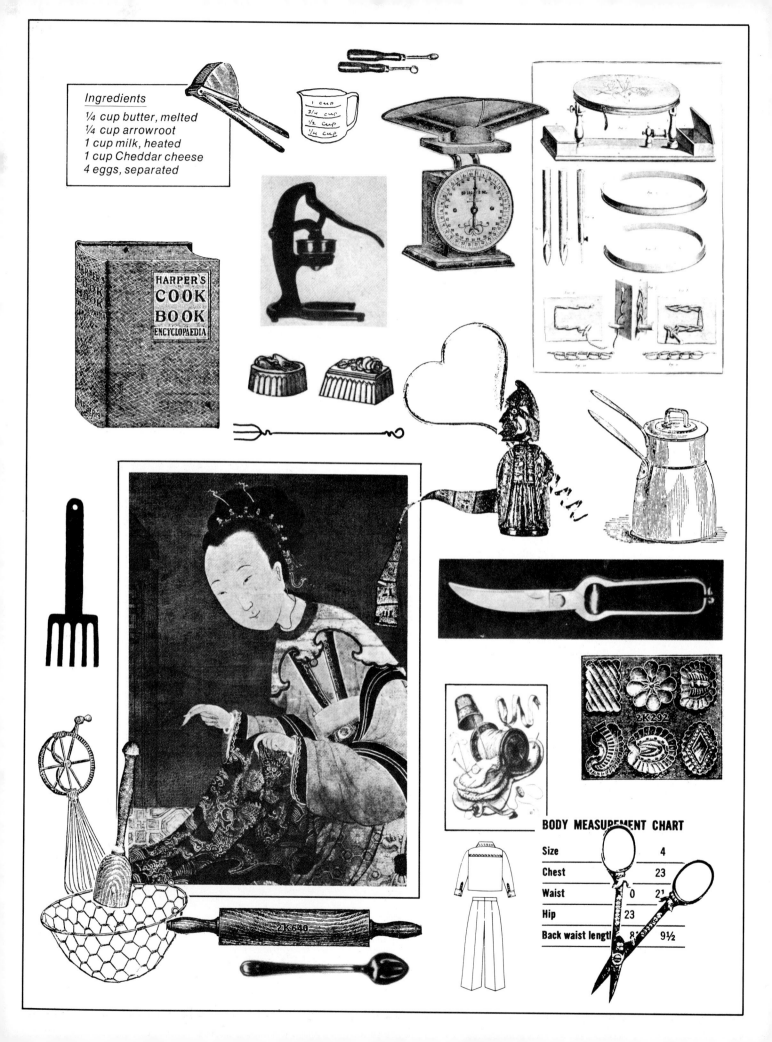

Ingredients

¼ cup butter, melted
¼ cup arrowroot
1 cup milk, heated
1 cup Cheddar cheese
4 eggs, separated

1 cup
¾ cup
½ cup
¼ cup

HARPER'S COOK BOOK ENCYCLOPAEDIA

2K 292

2K 640

BODY MEASUREMENT CHART

Size		4
Chest		23
Waist	0	2¹
Hip	23	
Back waist length	8¹	9½

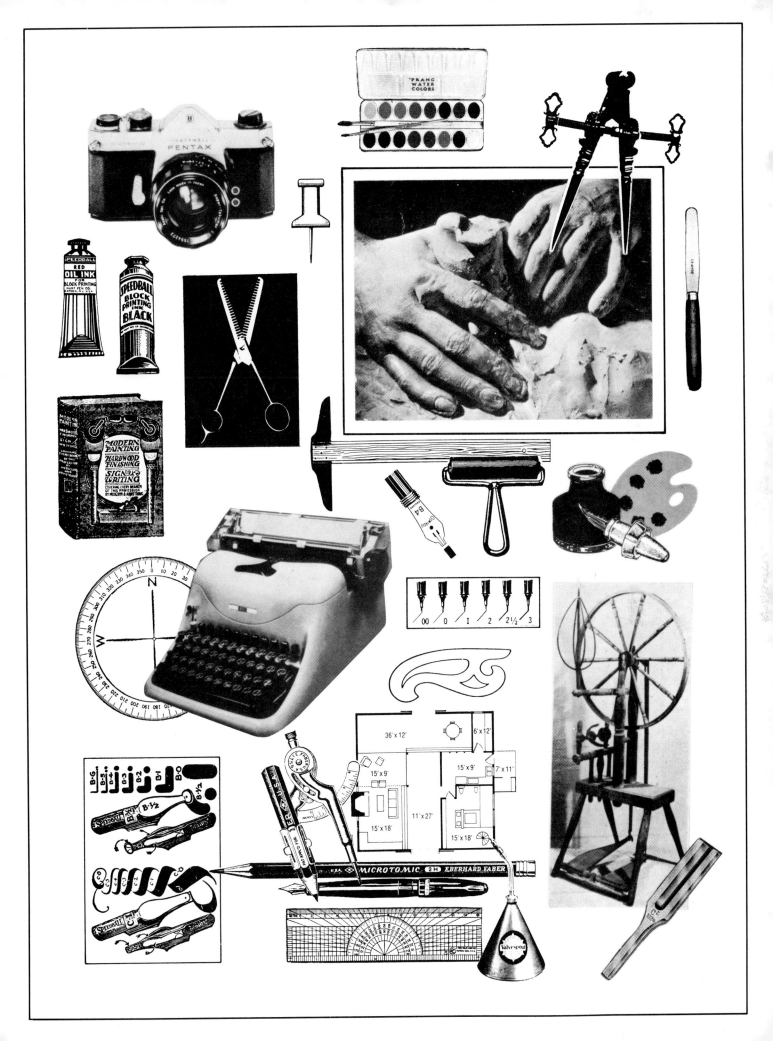

A ceremonial at a young ladies' seminary by an unknown artist, 1810

the domestic economy . . . supported a way of life centred upon the home, in which inner whims and compulsions were more obvious than external discipline. Each stage in industrial differentiation and specialisation struck also at the family economy, disturbing customary relations between man and wife, parents and children, and differentiating more sharply between "work" and "life." . . . The family was roughly torn apart each morning by the factory bell, and the mother who was also a wage-earner often felt herself to have the worst of both the domestic and the industrial worlds.

—E. P. Thompson, *The Making of the English Working Class*, 1963

WHY, woman wonders, does she continue to carry the cramp of deprivation, the sensation of her female exclusion from the wide world? She gnaws away at "the woman question."

So much of the trouble is because I am a woman. To me it seems a very terrible thing to be a woman. There is one crown which perhaps is worth it all—a great love, a quiet home, and children. We all know that is all that is worth while, and yet we must peg away, showing off our wares on the market if we have money, or manufacturing careers for ourselves if we haven't. We have not the motive to prepare ourselves for a "life-work" of teaching, of social work—we know that we would lay it down with hallelujah in the height of our success, to make a home for the right man. . . .

It is all so cruelly wasteful. There are so few ways in which we can compete with men—surely not in teaching or in social work. If we are not to have the chance to fulfill our one potentiality—the power of loving—why were we not born men? At least we could have had an occupation then. . . .

—Ruth Benedict, *Journal*, 1912

IN every century women discover their minds; like souls, these have no sex. Education, then, promises a paradise where the sexes together might graze equally and at will.

Neither arrogance nor presumption drives us to the audacity of wanting to be like God—that is, like man; we are not like Eve of old, lured by the beauty of the fruit of the tree of knowledge, nor does the snake encourage us to enjoy it. No, there has come to us something like a command; we are confronted with the necessity of biting into this apple, whether we think it good to eat or not, confronted with the fact that the paradise of naturalness and unconsciousness, in which many of us would too gladly tarry, is gone forever.

—Emma Jung, *Animus and Anima*, 1957

BUT there is no Eden.

A survey of *Women in Top Jobs* shows that even women who have achieved and persisted in high-level professional careers tend to side-step the confrontation with a man's world. They carve out for themselves specifically feminine roles which do not compete directly with those of their male colleagues . . .

The stress on sex equality appears self-delusory . . . the opening of the professions to women, the right of access they theoretically have to all forms of higher education, the opportunities which are now available to them for public, political and business careers—these are, for the vast majority of women in our society, mere visions. They represent what R. H. Tawney once described as "the impertinent courtesy of an invitation offered to unwelcome guests in the certainty that circumstances will prevent them from accepting it."

—Ann Oakley, *Woman's Work*, 1975

AND the fact of this sobering fact is often woman's hardest lesson to learn. Yet, women are, after all, mothers of invention.

Mother . . . I was telling somebody yesterday that the reason I am a poet is entirely because you wanted me to be and intended I should be, even from the very first. You brought me up in the tradition of poetry, and everything I did you encouraged. I can not remember once in my life when you were not interested in what I was working on, or even suggested that I should put it aside for something else. Some parents of children that are "different" have so much to reproach themselves with. But not you, Great Spirit.

—Edna St. Vincent Millay,
letter, June 15, 1921

AND like Eve and the daughters of Eve, cast out from Eden, women embrace the wide world and endeavor to live wisely in it.

But now I want to turn to . . . what can colleges do for the education of women? . . . A freshman study program that combines literature, sociology, psychology, and history would usefully introduce the subject to students; interdepartmental women's studies programs may be devised or particular courses (e.g., in the history of sociology of women) be added to existing departmental offerings. I value this curricular direction because it calls not for competition with men but for the growth of understanding by both men and women about how society is arranged. Such understanding is essential to intelligent action for social change as opposed to individual advancement.

—Florence Howe, "The Education of Women,"
Liberation, August-September 1969

SO WHEN you think that you are doing it alone—going back to school, or *going* to school, educating yourself to be a factory worker, lawyer, midwife, executive, physicist, beautician, plumber, welder, spy, senator, or feminist, remember: history teaches success, too.

I feel that the evolution of the totally free woman in our society will be possible only when we repossess the true dignity of our history and re-integrate it into our lives. Only then will we be able to move beyond this particular struggle, instead of being condemned to repeat it with each succeeding generation. The knowledge that my grandmother's contemporaries were not just good wives, mothers, housekeepers, and cooks but rather a generation of potentially revolutionary freedom fighters gives a new dimension to their lives and a new strength to mine.

—Midge Mackenzie,
Shoulder to Shoulder, 1975

Katherine Philips   Dorothy Osborne   Anne Countess of Winchelsea   Susannah Centlivre   Mrs. Manley   Catherine Cockburn   Mary B
Lydia Maria Child   Catherine Sedgwick   Catherine Beecher   Sarah J. Hale   Margaret Fuller   Harriet Beecher Stowe   Frances
Ann Hutchinson   Lucy Larcom   Kate Chopin   Jane Addams   Alice James   Mrs. Montagu   Fanny Burney   Sarah Trimm

THERE is a table laden. Some women already sit, faces from the past. They are assembled as though for a banquet. Places are laid for the women to come. This is the feast of women. These are the names of the feasters:

Mrs. Delaney   Sarah Fielding   Elizabeth Cellier   Hannah Glasse   Damaris Cudworth, Lady Masham   Laura Ingalls Wilder
a Gage   Julia Ward Howe   Louisa May Alcott   Elizabeth Palmer Peabody   Lydia Sigourney   Maria Mitchell   Anne Askew
Elizabeth Inchbald   Ann Radcliffe   Mrs. Norton   Mary Brunton   Elizabeth Hamilton   Mary Cassatt   Charlotte Yonge

THESE are the rituals and rites of this festival: hunger, a taste for learning, the education of the palate, and the skills to savor every concoction of woman's imaginative cooking and brewing. History offers us this, too—a company of women.

Susannah Annesley Wesley   Ann Baynard   Elizabeth Elstob   Lady Mary Wortley Montagu   Eliza Haywood   Charlotte Lennox   Elizabeth Carter   Florence Nightingale
Sarah Hackett Stevenson   Antoinette Brown Blackwell   Elizabeth Blackwell   Emma Stebbins   Sojourner Truth   Elizabeth Cady Stanton   Madame de la Fayette
Lucy Stone   Lucretia Mott   Susan B. Anthony   Francis E. Willard   Phebe A. Hanaford   Mercy B. Jackson   Susanna Wright   Phebe Cozzens   Pudentiana

Amelia Blumer   Augusta Miner   Hannah Adams   Lucile Desmoulins   Sophie de Condorcet   Zélide   George Sand   Marce
Bathsua Makin   Mary Astell   Mary Robinson   Anna Laetitia Barbauld   Charlotte Smith   Mary Wollstonecraft   Mary Hays   Ja
Anne Lady Bacon   Mary Stuart   Margaret Duchess of Newcastle   Anne Killigrew   Aphra Behn   Lady Pakington   Lady Chudle

I dared.
It was not God's proclamation.

—Sophocles, *Antigone*

Deborah   Abigail   Esther   Huldah   Miriam   Naomi   Ruth   Judith   Lucretia   Cornelia   Aspasia Hortensia   Dorcas   Lydia   Praxedes   Pudentiana   St. Radegunde   St. Hilda   St. Lioba   Hroswitha St. Hildegard   St. Herrad   Sappho   Juliana Barnes   Margaret, Countess of Richmond   Marie de France   Marie de Champagne   Beatrix de Dia   Christine de Pisan   Dame de Castelloza   Héloïse Pernett du Guillet   Louise Labe   Marguerite de Navarre   Helisenne de Crenne   Jeanne Flore Marguerite de Valois   Marie de Brabant   Madeleine de Scudery   Madame de la Fayette   Sévigné Comtesse de Murat   Ninon de Lenclose   Antoinette Deshoulière   Madame de Maintenon   Madame de Staël   Anne Boleyn   Margaret Roper   Anne Askew   Lady Jane Grey   Mary Tudor   Elizabeth I Mary Stuart   Anne Lady Bacon   Margaret Ascham   Lucy Hutchinson   Margaret Duchess of Newcastle   Lady Pakington   Anne Killigrew   Aphra Behn   Lady Chudleigh   Queen Isabella   Beatrix Galindo   Francisca de Lebrixa   Doña Maria Pacheco de Mendoza   Mary Sidney   Jane Weston   Lucrecia Marinelli   Marie de Jars   Anna van Schurman   Lady Bedford   Elisabeth Jocelyn   Lady Brilliana Harley   Letice Morison   Anna Hume   Mary Ward   Katherine Philips   Dorothy Osborne   Anne Countess of Winchelsea   Susannah Centlivre   Mrs. Manley   Catherine Cockburn   Mary Beale   Mrs. Delaney   Sarah Fielding   Elizabeth Cellier   Hannah Glasse   Damaris Cudworth, Lady Masham Susannah Annesley Wesley   Ann Baynard   Elizabeth Elstob   Lady Mary Wortley Montagu   Eliza Haywood   Charlotte Lennox   Elizabeth Carter   Bathsua Makin   Mary Astell   Mary Robinson   Anna Laetitia Barbauld   Charlotte Smith   Mary Wollstonecraft   Mary Hays   Jane West   Catharine Macauley   Anna Seward   Helen Maria Williams   Hester Lynch Thrale   Hannah More   Jane Austen Felicia Hemans   Mme. Roland   Olympe de Gouges   Pocahontas   Phillis Wheatley   Anne Bradstreet Abigail Adams   Lydia Maria Child   Catherine Sedgwick   Catherine Beecher   Sarah J. Hale   Margaret Fuller   Harriet Beecher Stowe   Frances Dana Gage   Julia Ward Howe   Louisa May Alcott Elizabeth Palmer Peabody   Lydia Sigounrey   Maria Mitchell   Sarah Hackett Stevenson   Antoinette Brown Blackwell   Elizabeth Blackwell   Emma Stebbins   Sojourner Truth   Elizabeth Cady Stanton Lucy Stone   Lucretia Mott   Susan B. Anthony   Francis E. Willard   Phebe A. Hanaford   Mercy B. Jackson   Susanna Wright   Phebe Cozzens   Amelia Blumer   Augusta Miner   Hannah Adams   Lucile Desmoulins   Sophie de Condorcet   Zélide   George Sand   Marceline Desbordes-Valmore   Juliette Drouet   Caroline Wuiet   Flora Tristan   Suzanne Voilquin   George Eliot   Charlotte Brontë Emily Brontë   Carrie Chapman Catt   Angelina Grimke   Sarah Grimke   Christabel Pankhurst Emily Dickinson   Amy Lowell   Ann Hutchinson   Lucy Larcom   Mary Boykin Chestnut   Mary Putnam Jacobi   Kate Chopin   Jane Addams   Alice James   Mrs. Montagu   Fanny Burney   Sarah Trimmer   Elizabeth Inchbald   Ann Radcliffe   Mrs. Norton   Mary Brunton   Elizabeth Hamilton Mary Cassatt   Angelica Kauffman   Elizabeth Gaskell   Florence Nightingale   Clara Barton   Mary Wollstonecraft Shelley   Charlotte Yonge   Lucy Sprague Montgomery   Laura Ingalls Wilder   Emmeline Pankhurst   Sylvia Pankhurst

Every woman has a history
Mother and grandmother and the ones be-
    fore that
the faces she sees in her dreams or visions
And wonders Who?

Each one is queen, mother, huntress
though each remembers little of it
And some remember nothing at all . . .

Let go from there, start over,
Live it again, until she knows who she is,
Until she rises as though from the sea . . .
a woman big-hipped, beautiful, and fierce.

—Sharon Barba, "A Cycle of Women," 1973

Cosmetic Cosmology

Went into a shoe store to buy a pair of shoes,
There was a shoe salesman humming the blues
Under his breath; over his breath
Floated a peppermint lifesaver, a little wreath.

I said please I need a triple-A
And without stopping humming or swallowing his lifesaver away
He gave one glance from toe to toe
And plucked from the mezzanine the very shoe.

Skill of the blessed, that at their command
Blue and breathless comes to hand
To send, from whatever preoccupation, feet
Implacably shod into the perfect street.

—Josephine Miles, "Sale," 1960

CHICKEN LITTLE

CACKLE, cackle, see those birdbrains scratching around the bargain basement bins. Out shopping, buying, and spending—country-mousewife, spangled hooker, corporate spouse, high society queen bee—women are all scavengers of self-décor. A woman purchases her identity every time she walks out her door— with shopping list in hand—to the facialist, the plastic surgeon, the neighborhood beauty

When vulgarly extravagant, or poor, or clumsy, or careless about her acts of decoration, woman is a tasteless fowl. Men—and lots of women—grunt: "She's a pig" or a cow, or a horse, or a bitch in heat. When she can make herself look good, we see her and drool, and call woman fox, filly, bunny, pussycat, butterfly. And so women flit from store to store, counter to counter, style to style, fashion to fashion, trying on, turning out, tearing off versions of themselves.

parlor, the January clearance sale, the Woolworth's cosmetics counter, the weight doctor, the fancy fat farm, the jeweler, the shoe store, the corsetorium, the dressmaker, the perfumery, the tattoo artist, the bust builder, the pedicurist, the electrolysist, the masseuse.

Women waste their lives in the activities of ornamentation: preening, ruffling, licking, stroking, smoothing, poking—like hens (or toothsome chicks)—pecking mindlessly in the barnyard of beautification.

There is a passion for dress and ornament nowadays which has probably never been surpassed. Monsieur Worth has recently stated that in the middle of [the nineteenth century] women of high fashion went through the Season with two silk dresses and a cashmere shawl. To dress well today partakes of the nature of a fine art, and demands as much time, study and capital from

its devotees as the steady pursuit of an artistic career. These dresses of course must be shown and hence the modern feminine craze for living, as it were, in public . . .

—*Lady's Companion*, March 10, 1900

Mrs. Washington was extremely plain in her dress. . . . At a ball given in New Jersey in honor to herself, she wore a 'simple russet gown,' and white handkerchief about her neck, thereby setting an example to the women of the Revolution who could ill afford to spend their time or means as lavishly as they might have desired.

—Phoebe Hanaford,
Daughters of America, 1848

Don't ask me what to wear

I have no embroidered
headband from Sardis to
give you, Cleis, such as
I wore
       and my mother
always said that in her
day a purple ribbon
looped in the hair was thought
to be high style indeed

but we were dark:

         a girl
whose hair is yellower than
torchlight should wear no
headdress but fresh flowers

       —Sappho, Fragment 83

ONCE upon a time, a woman had to look her best; what that was she was not quite sure—it certainly wasn't what she was now; no. The most obvious problem was her hair. It seemed simple to go to an expensive salon (or just around the corner maybe because that would be fast) to look somehow the way she was supposed to. Or wanted to. Or would, if she had the time. Yes, the hairdresser, the dresser of hair. So to the shop. Negotiations start: perm, straighten, dye ("No, dear, tint"), pluck, tease, cut, curl, shape, bake. Compromise: not the newest or the latest, but at least what's right for her. Result: herself refashioned for the public eye. Why? Mostly women don't know why; lots of women hate having to spend the time and money and energy putting themselves together.

Clothes were a problem, too. The black market both offended our consciences and was far beyond the reach of our purse; but the official ration of clothing coupons was stingy in the extreme. I got hold of some after my father's death, enough to let me get a dress and overcoat made, which I took great care of. Toward the end of autumn many women exchanged their skirts for slacks, which kept one much warmer, and I followed their example; except when I was going to the lycée, my outdoor costume consisted of skiing rig, complete with boots. I had enjoyed keeping up my personal appearance in the days when such activities formed a pleasurable diversion; but I had no wish now to burden my existence with pointless complications of this sort, and so I stopped bothering. It already demanded considerable effort to keep up a decent minimum of appearance.

—Simone de Beauvoir,
The Prime of Life, 1960

BUT women's appetites seem here to rule them; they have to. Though plucked and featherless, women are hens who need a steady supply of grubs—perfume, shoes, necklaces, paints, furs, belts, stockings, brassieres, scarves, boots, hairpieces, dresses, blouses, sweaters, skirts, suits, hats, gloves—things to adorn themselves with. And for many women, this search for adornment is the business of their lives.

Unlike the female of other species, woman-animal must pursue her furs, her feathers, her claws, her scents. She must work to be fashionably female. The lioness lies licking her beautiful coat; woman goes in mad pursuit of mink, lynx, sable, even rabbit skins. All her life long, woman pursues, as well, tantalizing, arbitrary images of herself. Woman's public female beauty is not given by nature; it is learned by rote.

A girl named Gayle, a dentist's daughter from New Jersey, was given a nose job and a fox stole for graduation from high school by her father. Her mother wanted him to give Gayle a mink but he resisted, mother yelped, until he reminded her that if he gave Gayle a mink, what would there be for her future husband to give her? Every Friday night at school we used to watch her—for an *hour*—she was doing her face: for an hour! When she swept out in contact lenses and the fox stole we used to wonder whether that hour would pay off. End of story: Gayle finished exams, the only Freshman with a four carat pear-shaped diamond ring. So it paid off, I guess.

WOMEN's education is certainly different from men's. Women have seldom through time been intimate with the motions of planets—astronomy; the reproductive life of the newt—biology; the routes taken by rats in a maze—psychology; the number of angels dancing on the head of a pin—theology. But women have always possessed their own science, cosmetic cosmology. Like the students of any science, women study the vocabulary of this cosmology, memorize its rules, experiment with its skills, aspire to its arts. Woman's art, women's science—true domestic science—is the pattern on face and dress and ass. Ask any woman and she'll name her best feature, she'll *know* how to decorate it. She knows that her world, her cosmos, is cosmetics. And she'll agree that clothes may make the man, but woman *is* the world she wears.

> I secured my stockings with black garters. I moistened my lips; their painted surface glistened. I powdered the flanges of my nostrils and removed a superfluous hair from my chin. I mopped and mowed, inspected eyes for offensive rheums and teeth for odious sores. I tousled my hair. My nerves were sharp. My eyes smarted under their heavy load. I composed my expression. I stared into the glass three feet away. Certainly, I thought, I have an intellectual face.
>
> —Norma Meacock, *Thinking Girl*, 1968

> When anyone speaks of her beauty she says that she never was beautiful, although she had that reputation thirty years ago. Nevertheless, she speaks of her beauty as often as she can.
>
> —Monsieur de Maisse discusses the Queen, 1597

FROM BARNYARD TO JUNGLE

Every barnyard, big or small, has its pecking order, a set of prudent rules by which its inhabitants live alongside each other and survive. So women share with each other tactics for self-decoration, design, disguise—
> mothers take their daughters shopping;
> sisters hand down outworn clothes;
> together, friends practice the latest fads of hair and nails and eyes.

There's always been a community of effort to spread the word.

> Martha desires her best love, & will be happy to welcome any letter from you. . . . She is pleased with my Gown, & particularly bids me say that if you could see me in it for five minutes, she is sure you would be eager to make up your own. . . .
>
> —Jane Austen,
> letter, Sunday, November 30, 1800

> Great Nature clothes the soul, which is but thin,
> With fleshly garments, which the Fates do spin,
> And when these garments are grown old and bare,
> With sickness torn, Death takes them off with care,
> And folds them up in peace and quiet rest,
> And lays them safe within an earthly chest:
> Then scours them well and makes them sweet and clean,
> Fit for the soul to wear those clothes again.
>
> —Margaret Cavendish,
> Duchess of Newcastle,
> "The Soul's Garments," 1653

BUT women are female beasts as well as thinking animals. Dress, decoration, design all transform them into beasts of prey. Scavenger turns predator; fickle hen goes hunting. Magically, ally is enemy: now the meat they pant for is the envy of other women; the hunt they lust for is the imitation of other women; the

Ye meaner beauties I permit ye shine;
Go, triumph in the hearts that once were
    mind;
But 'midst your triumphs with confusion
    know,
'Tis to my ruin all your arms ye owe.
Would pitying heaven restore my wonted
    mien,
Ye still might move unthought of and un-
    seen;
But oh, how vain, how wretched is the boast
Of beauty faded, and of empire lost!
What now is left but weeping, to deplore
My beauty fled, and empire now no more?

—Lady Mary Wortley Montagu,
"Saturday the Small Pox," 1763

satisfaction the most savage women crave is domination. Where else can women dominate each other? Not on battlefields, or in banks, or learned councils, or factories, or legislatures, or industries of fashion which are run by men, not even on school boards. But in every hamlet, village, town, housing development and project, and high rise, every nook and cranny of female life, one woman is making another woman feel bad because—

she's the best dressed
she's the chicest
she's the smartest
she's the prettiest

or

she's got peaches-and-cream skin
she's got great boobs
she's got silky legs
she's got shiny hair

and, and, and . . .

WHOEVER she is, wherever she lives, she has the power to make other women look and feel terrible. She has the potency to force homage from other women.

WOMAN's world is the universe of appearance. Costume, style, shape, color, taste, décor— a woman manipulates these to wrest power and prestige from other women. If fashion is frivolous, dress, for women, is dominion.

No woman ever really *dresses* for a man—men like their women undressed. For men, the naked female animal has fur and smell and secretion and flush enough. A woman never feels herself more beautiful than after getting out of bed with a lover: her nakedness dresses her then.

A sweet disorder in the dress
Kindles in clothes a wantonness. . . .
A careless shoestring, in whose tie
I see a wild civility;—
Do more bewitch me, than when art
Is too precise in every part.

—Robert Herrick,
"Delight in Disorder," 1648

So WOMEN only dress for other women. They dress to kill. And in the life of woman as she confronts the eyes of other women there are three epochs of destructiveness, three targets of aggression, three categories of adversary.

As a girl, a female fights to displease her mother. She puts on too much make-up, or too little; wears a white brassiere under a black sweater, streaks her hair until it turns green, or dyes it until all the brushes go black; raids her mother's drawers for stockings, rings, perfume, purses. She and her mother are locked in combat. And in that public battle zone—the department store— the two of them create squalid spectacles, refereed by patient sales ladies, over the purchase of tight pants, clinging sweaters, see-through blouses, flashy colors, tortuous shoes.

Watch this girl grow. See her become a veteran warrior in fierce struggle with other women. Now she arms herself to capture and ravish other women's men. Now her preparation for battle is studied and serious; whatever the rules of current fashion she must spend hours elbowing other women away and choosing the best artillery.

At last, older, wiser, the female of the species dresses to annoy other women.

SUCH is the lawless jungle of predatory females: strip the hen, see the cat, watch the claws scratch.

CINDERELLA'S STEPSISTERS

There once was an ugly duckling
With feathers all scruffy and brown
And the other birds in so many words
Said: "khurum—get out of town."

—"The Ugly Duckling"

CATTY women say: Look at those stretch marks on her stomach—Did you notice how lined her face is now?—She's let herself go to the dogs with those extra twenty pounds— How can a young girl let herself get so fat—

She should never wear pants with a bottom like that—If only she'd cut her hair her face wouldn't look so pinched—Somebody should take her in hand. And the ugly duckling shudders. If in the eyes of the flock she's blemished, woman is chased out of town. Tyrannical, mean, vicious, critical—we can all be crows whose pleasure it is to hurt other females. Each of us does this. Each of us knows it can be done to us—that fat ass, pinched by a man, will be clawed by another woman. Why?

In the arena of appearance, women's violence—selective in other places—is on display, uniformed, attired, invested with power.

One's appearance, a lifetime of effort put into improving that, most of it ill judged. Only neatness is vital now, and one can

finally live like a humble but watchful ghost. . . . In very truth the old are almost free . . .

—Florida Scott-Maxwell,
The Measure of My Days, 1968

WOMEN'S tongues—their most ancient weapon for violence—stands on guard, ready to do slashing savagery. Women are meddling butchers, carving up their own kind. And, like all mercenaries, their uniforms *are* what they fight for: one look at another woman tells us who she is, where she comes from, how much money she has to spend on herself, which pack she runs with. We scent instantly whether we will have to defend ourselves against her, or charge her, or whether we belong to the same herd. And so to avoid the pain of being the ugly duckling, women often run in defensive packs; they herd to fend off the aggressive eye and tongue of other women. There's always safety in numbers.

A footman, with long experience in upper-class households, said "jewellery was a badge that women wore like a sergeant major's stripes or field-mahshal's baton, it showed achievement, rank, position."

—Ernest King, *The Green Baize Door*, 1963
(quoted in Leonore Davidoff,
The Best Circles, 1973)

Old Money looking at New: "Too bad she can't find another place on her body to stick another dollar bill."
New Money looking at Old: "You can never get them to part with a penny and they look it."

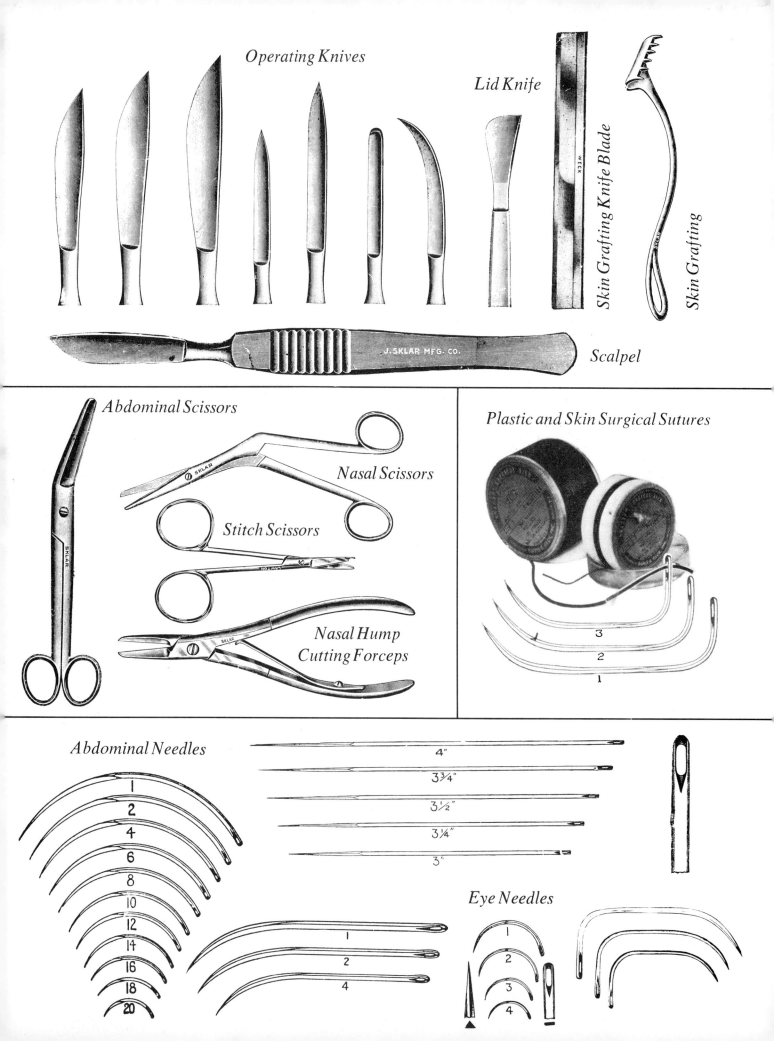

Operating Knives

Lid Knife

Skin Grafting Knife Blade

Skin Grafting

Scalpel

J. SKLAR MFG. CO.

Abdominal Scissors

Nasal Scissors

Stitch Scissors

Nasal Hump
Cutting Forceps

Plastic and Skin Surgical Sutures

3
2
1

Abdominal Needles

1
2
4
6
8
10
12
14
16
18
20

4"
3¾"
3½"
3¼"
3"

1
2
4

Eye Needles

1
2
3
4

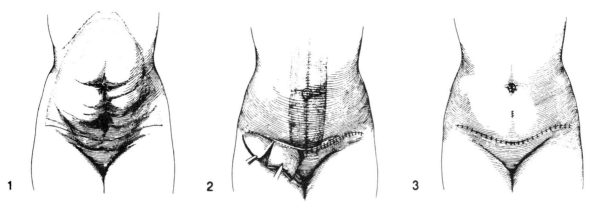

1. *Drawing of a patient with flabby abdomen caused either by frequent pregnancies, or by sudden weight loss.*
2. *The skin is cut around the navel and undermined up to the ribs.*
3. *Before closing the wound, the navel's new position is calculated.*

WOMEN will do nearly anything not to be the ugly duckling, the runt of the litter, the outcast.

"You cannot believe how materialistic Flatbush was. All anybody in my high school thought about was the material requirements for popularity: clothes, jewelry. . . . Girls could tell what label dress you were wearing simply by glancing at you. . . . Everyone had to look like a carbon copy of the next person. After one Easter holiday, five girls came back to school with the exact same nose job."

—*Woman's Fate: Raps from a Feminist Consciousness Raising Group,* 1973

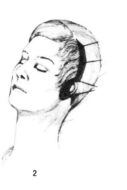

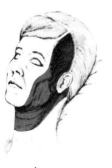

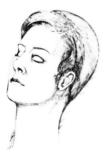

1. *First stage of a face-lift. The hair is parted, and an incision is made starting about three centimeters behind the widow's peak and extending downward above the ear. The incision continues down in front of the ear, curves around the earlobe and upward behind the ear, and finally turns backward toward the neck hairline. The dotted line indicates the extent of the undermining of the skin, which varies considerably from patient to patient, depending on the extent of the wrinkles.*

2. *The skin is rotated upward and backward, and the amount of excess skin is calculated. The dotted line indicates the eventual suture line.*

3. *Final stage of the same face-lift. An anchor suture is placed above the ear and another behind it. The wound is then sutured all along with a fine thread, with special care to avoid tension on the skin around the earlobe, for this results in an unattractive downward pull.*

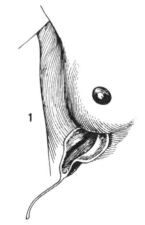

1. *Through a five-centimeter incision on the breast fold the empty folded balloon implant is inserted behind the mammary gland.*

2. *A variable amount of saline solution is injected into the implant through a small tube, which is then trimmed and sealed.*

3. *The wound is sutured.*

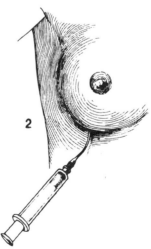

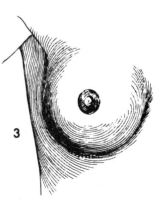

Mirror, mirror, on the wall
Who is the fairest one of all?

THE story goes that beneath the rags Cinderella was beautiful. A simple wave of a generous
godmother's wand easily revealed Cinderella's
innate loveliness. For her stepsisters, however,
beauty is labor—it requires more than the
wave of a wand or the touch of a tight small
glass slipper. Big, short, small, fat, meager,
messy, most of us are caught in the cross fire
of cosmetic aggression.

Towards the beginning of the present century, it seems to have been the prevailing
opinion, that nature had made the female
waist greatly too large; to remedy which the
stiffest stays were laced on in the tightest
manner, lest the young ladies should become clumsy, or grow crooked. Towards the
middle of the century, it began to be discovered, that besides the uneasiness of such
a situation, it frequently produced the very
effects it was intended to prevent; physicians and philosophers now declaimed
against stays, and they were by many laid
aside with such abhorrence that the fashion
took quite a different turn. We discovered
that our mothers had all been in the wrong,
and that nature had not made the female
waist nearly so large as it ought to have been;

but the ladies supplied this defect so well with clothes, that about the years 1759 and 1760 every woman, old and young, had the appearance of being big with child. In ten or twelve years the fashion began to take the opposite direction again, and small waists are esteemed so great a beauty, that, in endeavouring to procure them, women have outdone all the efforts of their grandmothers in the beginning of the century. . . .

—W. Alexander, *History of Women*, 1779

WHATEVER else they do or do not do, women always work at decorating themselves.

To be born woman is to know—
Although they do not talk of it at school—
That we must labour to be beautiful.

—W. B. Yeats, "Adam's Curse," 1903

WHILE other women have to steal time to refurbish themselves—daily, hourly, yearly—actresses and prostitutes work steadily at this and are paid for this work. And so they have often been the advance guard in deciding how respectable women will look somewhat later. This time lag depends always on how much society cares about the distinction between the good woman and the bad, between the private woman and the public woman, between the woman in the home and the woman on the streets.

The house is for the good woman, the street is for the bad.

—Meander, fifth century

SOMETIMES, in fact all too often, the tricks of the public woman's trade, her arsenal of artifice, is adopted and adapted by a good woman. For a long time painted women were considered creatures of the streets, for it was only prostitutes and actresses who experimented with the arts and sciences of paint for hair and face. So if, let us say, in 1910, a law-abiding woman dyed her hair, or wore rouge, or tinted her toenails, wouldn't she have become one of the band of lawless, venal women she was meant to despise? What could respectable women do about graying hair, for example, or fading lips, or dried-up toenails without

being socially compromised? Commerce, the big business of fashion, has long known how to package and promote and make "tasteful" the appetites of women. So, recognizing the paradox of paint and painting in the lives of good women—all of whom could be counted on to grow old—big business created a new kind of fairy godmother for Cinderella's stepsisters, applying advanced technology to the religion of physical transcendence. In 1930 Clairol introduced hair dyes ("No, dear, tints") for the use of the average, good woman. In 1928 Elizabeth Arden packaged face colors, assuring women everywhere around the globe that everyone else was using them. Magically, the painted Jezebel became the woman of taste.

You see the outlines of her limbs quite clearly through the cloud of muslin veiling which surrounds her. Some sweet fools who have the reputation of good taste, are enchanted at the sight of the half-covered charms, and admire aloud these naked graces, lifting their round fleshy shoulders in fiery rhapsody, praising the treacherous witchery of her full dainty bust and the symmetry of her limbs; and you will see how other hateful beauties, believing that they, in order to have grace imputed to them and to attract universal admiration, have only to change their thick clothes for a muslim cloud, will in a few days fill the fashionable promenades of New Bond Street, Pall Mall, Hyde Park, Kensington Gardens, etc., with crowds of half-naked figures. When a cutting north-east wind blows, cold, illness, and death are brought with the sharp air to the thinly clothed bodies; the beauties shiver with cold, but fashion will not have it otherwise, and doctors, chemists, and gravediggers reckon on a good harvest.

—J. C. Huttner, *Pictures of London Manners and Morals*, 1801

AND so the combat in the cosmetic zone continues. While the battle rages within the community of women, those makers of sophisticated arms—Fabergé, Charles of the Ritz, Revlon, Avon, Maybelline, Coty, Helena Rubinstein, Chanel—escalate the war.

In all the time since I began making up and giving beauty treatments to so many women of my own age, I have never yet encountered a fifty-year-old woman who has lost heart, or a sixty-year-old suffering from nerves. It is among these lady champions that it does one good to attempt—and to bring to fruition—miracles. Where are those rouges of yesteryear, with their harsh redcurrant tints, those ungrateful whites, those Virgin Mary blues? We now have a range of tints at our disposal that would go to the head of a painter. The art of improving faces, and its ally, the cosmetic industry, now have a yearly turnover almost as large as that of the motion-picture industry. The harder the times are for women, the more determined women become, and proudly so, to hide the suffering it inflicts on them. . . . I have never felt so much esteem for woman, or so much admiration, as in the time I have been seeing her at such close quarters, since I have been holding, tilted back beneath my blue metallic rays, her faced stripped of its secrets, rich with expression, so various beneath its agile wrinkles, or new once more and refreshed for having for a moment relinquished its added tints. Oh, brave fighters! It is the fight itself that keeps you young.

—Colette, *Earthly Paradise*, 1966

BUT war is war. And so there are voices and forces always reminding women to be better than their bestial, predatory selves. These voices say: It is wrong and wasteful and bad to spend so much time, so much energy, so much money dressing up. They say:

The love of dress, which thou dost hate and despise in the women of the world who come to thee, has grown apace on earth, and has become a madness, and brings down the wrath of God. [Women] delight in walking about, their steps hampered by the mass of their garments, they try to wear out to no profit what the poor sorely need. O wretchedness, O blindness!

—St. Elisabeth of Schonau, twelfth century

I will in like manner, also, that women adorn themselves in modest apparel, with shamefacedness and sobriety: not with broidered hair or gold, or pearls, or costly array; but, which becometh women professing godliness, with good works.

—St. Paul: 1 Tim. ii. 8, 10

—And did they pursue a plan of conduct and not waste their time in following the fashionable vagaries of dress, the management of their household and children need not shut [women] out from literature, or prevent their attaching themselves to a science with that steady eye which strengthens the mind, or practising one of the fine arts that cultivate the taste.

—Mary Wollstonecraft,
The Rights of Woman, 1792

ARMED TRUCE

BEAUTY may kill, but fashion can educate. It is a university as well as a jungle. And as a school, its libraries are filled with learned journals, those despised relations of journalism—women's magazines. Though often regarded as trivial, women's magazines have always educated and neutralized the warfare within the community of women. The first women's magazine in America—*The Ladies Magazine and Repository* (Philadelphia, 1792)—was already allied with the community of women; in fact, it even advertised the communal vision of Mary Wollstonecraft's feminist manifesto, *A Vindication of the Rights of Woman* published earlier in the same year. The first women's magazine in England—*The Ladies' Mercury* (1693)—opened to the female reading public "all the most nice and curious Questions concerning Love, Marriage, Behaviour, Dress, and Humor of the Female Sex, whether Virgins, Wives or Widows."

Like the women's novel, the ladies' magazines referee the public exchange of information among women. In the absence of serious, formal education for women—indeed in the vacuum created by its prohibition—these magazines maintain a network of lore growing out of and cultivating all the aspects of that domestic science, cosmetic cosmology, so important to their women readers.

The didactic influence of the ladies' magazines is their single most important feature; they appeared during the eighteenth century as female literacy increased dramatically. Like their sister, female fiction, they were conceived in the promise of intellectual liberty, dedicated to the proposition that women might someday "not hesitate to store their minds with useful knowledge through the fear of being called masculine" (*Lady Amaranth*, 1838). Mrs. Susannah Rowson, one of the early leaders of women's journalism, borrowed an idea from contemporary political feminism—the "rights of women"—to vindicate women's rights to all "that useful knowledge" which she hoped to impart to her readers. She wrote:

> We assert our right for tis our pride
> In all domestic matters to preside
> And on the mystery of rising pies

Compounding soups and stews philosophize . . .
Are fathers, brothers, friends, oppressed with care,
We claim a right in all their grief to share,
It is our right to watch the sick man's bed
Bathe the swolen limb and bind the aching head.
These rights we may assert and however common
These, and these only, are the rights of woman.

—*The Boston Weekly Magazine* (1801)

HERE we can see the blueprint for women's magazines which has, in fact, already been in force for a hundred years. This same pattern continues into the present. Any contemporary reader of *Vogue, Ladies Home Journal, Queen, Elle, Nova, Ms.* would instantly feel at home in the pages of similar British journals.

Their formula is always the same. With few exceptions, women readers can, as they

could, expect to find both entertainment and instruction in pages devoted to "Society, Literature, Art, Morals, Health, Fashion, and Domestic Happiness," including, of course, the tactics of dress and the stratagems of fashionable success. Among pages devoted to "A Mother's Department, Hints for Housekeepers, a Health Department, a Work Table, and colored fashion plates," domestic science in these magazines inevitably includes the cultivation of taste and the mind. Some magazines, like *Arthur's Ladies' Magazine of Elegant Literature and the Fine Arts* (1844), attempted to cultivate literary taste in their readers by reviewing and recommending current literature, and by encouraging and *publishing* the literary efforts of their readers. When narrowly focused in this way, periodicals for women could never gain the readership of a *Godey's* or a *Good Housekeeping*

centering on the how-to's of fashion, health, and home.

Teaching is, of course, the heart of the women's magazine: it nourishes the concerns of women. It pacifies rather than panders to women's appetites; it neutralizes rather than negates women's wars; it celebrates rather than castigates that inner beauty we all, like Cinderella, believe lies waiting to be discovered.

And so, like Cinderella's stepsisters, we labor. Despite all our resentment at being manipulated by style-setters, at having our tastes and our faces prefabricated and dictated to and pummeled, despite all our chagrin at the impossibility (and wastefulness) of those costumes we wear, despite all our anger at the contagion of conspicuous consumption, despite all our discomfort at the pleasure the pursuit of fashion brings, we do labor to be beautiful.

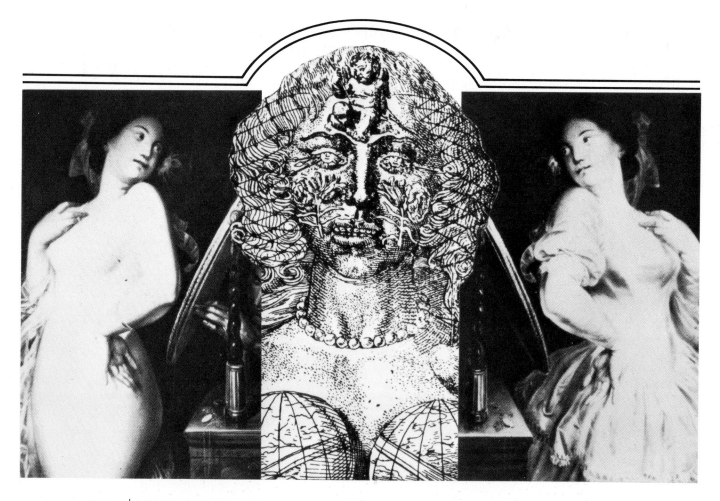

She maketh herself coverings of tapestry;
Her clothing is silk and purple. . . .
Strength and honour are her clothing;
And she shall rejoice in time to come. . . .
Give her of the fruit of her hands;
And let her own works praise her in the gates.

—"Praise of a Good Woman," Proverbs, 31

THE SINGLE LIFE

Solo

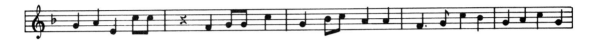

I never will marry, I'll be no man's wife,
And I shall live single for the rest of my life. —American ballad

THE SINGLE WOMAN. Hers is a hidden and puzzling life. She is always asked: Why didn't you marry? The married woman is never asked: why *did* you? But married women often spend time thinking about being single. It seems an enchanted state: freedom, indulgence—who you want, what you want, when you want, how you want. In that land of unattachment there are no whining children; morning sleep stretches out well past eleven o'clock; hungry husbands never belch, wanting food when *they* want it; you travel alone—without bulging bags you arrive on the Costa del Sol, in Paris, Puerto Rico, tanned or not, beautiful in and out of season, to find that dressing alone *can* take hours and hours; and nights are for the freelance of sex.

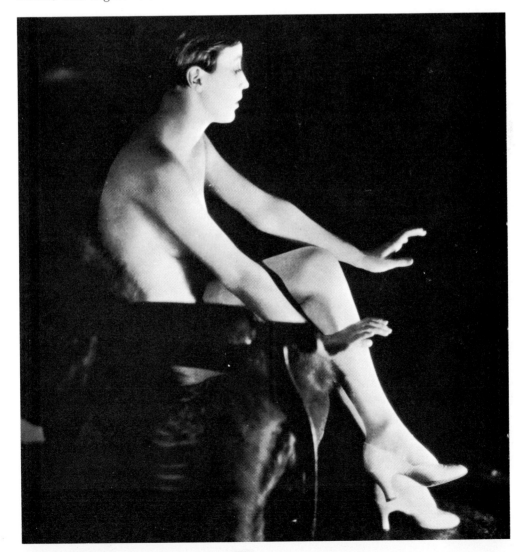

NO MAN'S WIFE

The other woman
Finds time to manicure her nails
The other woman
Is perfect where her rival fails
And she's never seen with pincurls in her
  hair
The other woman
Enchants her clothes with french perfume
The other woman
Keeps fresh cut flowers in each room
There are never toys scattered anywhere
And when her man comes to call
He'll find her waiting like a lonesome queen
Cuz when she's by his side
It's such a change from old routine.

> —Nina Simone, "The Other Woman"

SINGLE women also spend time thinking about being single. They know they possess their own time, their own money, their own lease, their own car and keys. When business or pleasure calls them away, they can go—and for days. If men take them, they take men too and sometimes turn them out.

If pretty, clever or shrewd enough, the woman alone is the world's guest. She flirts, she parties, she is given gifts—speedboats, tape decks, plane tickets, and all the meals she can eat. When the tables turn and she hosts, she manages with skill the carving knife, the music, the corkscrew and the bed. Why then do we wonder why single women remain single?

Who's gonna shoe your pretty little foot?
Who's gonna glove your hand?
Who's gonna kiss your red ruby lips?
Who's gonna be your man?

Poppa's gonna shoe my pretty little foot.
Momma's gonna glove my hand.
Sister's gonna kiss my red ruby lips.
And I don't need no man.

> —ballad

BUT we do wonder why a woman stays alone. Because, of course, mothers want weddings and grandchildren; sisters want a home away from home; fathers want to stop financing charge accounts, dental bills, and insurance payments; the men in the office really want to get back to work; students want the riddle solved—what's she wearing the black brassiere for, if she's not getting it regular; and friends want a safe happiness for her and themselves.

And then, if she stays single, we worry and we wonder. Though we're too embarrassed to ask, we want to know: What does she do for sex, and does she have too much or not enough. And we look at her face and see where it's aging and we're certain that there will be nobody to love her because those lines can only cut deeper. So we try to explain her single life. And then we call single woman: spinster, lesbian, fag bag, nympho, old maid, mousy librarian, gym teacher, career woman, betrayed mistress, misfit, dutiful daughter, dreamer. We believe her life will be forever frozen into those patterns of female solitude: virgin, governess, feminist, nun, blues singer, actress, slut, prostitute, outcast.

The other woman
Will always cry herself to sleep,
Will never have his love to keep,
And as the years go by
The other woman
Will spend her life
Alone.

> —Nina Simone, "The Other Woman"

WE think the woman alone bereft of life. We pity her, we also dislike her.

Let me tell you a little story
About Miss Edith Gee;
She lived in Clevedon Terrace
At Number 83.

She's a slight squint in her left eye,
Her lips they were thin and small,
She had narrow sloping shoulders
And she had no bust at all.

She'd a velvet hat with trimmings,
And a dark-grey serge costume;
She lived in Clevedon Terrace
In a small bed-sitting room.

> —W. H. Auden, "Miss Gee," 1937

YET at the same time, we understand that the single woman's liberty is subversive. With all that time on her hands, with all those perfumed dresses, she's probably up to some mischief, whatever her age. And so we watch her with suspicion. We mistrust her: she may suddenly become a sexual magnet, drawing other women's men after her.

WORSE still, the single woman threatens to become a dangerous charm, seducing a man's woman from her proper place. No man wants his woman with another woman, leagued against him, bewitched with her tales of freedom. No man likes to be the main course at a woman's luncheon—call it a consciousness-raising group or a quilting bee; anyway, a single woman can only side with his wife when she flaps her tongue and tells spicy tales about him.

> Woman, I don't want a soul hanging round
>   my house
> When I'm not at home.
> Don't want you to answer the door
> For nobody.
> When you home and you all alone.
> Don't want your sister coming by,
> Cuz the little girl she talk too much . . .
>
> —J. Johnson, "Don't Answer the Door"

BUT for both men and women the single life is an alternative to a joint life with another. When men choose this avenue, we shrug our shoulders; when women live it—without mate, or marriage—we don't understand why. Single women, then, carry a secret, pose a question whose answer we can only guess at. We always wonder why they remain single.

Average U.S. Household Drops
Below 3 Persons for First Time

WASHINGTON, July 6 (AP)—For the first time in American history the average household consists of fewer than three persons, and the Census Bureau says this is part of a basic change in how Americans live and how they relate to each other.

A report released last week told of a declining marriage rate, an increasing divorce rate, a continued low birth rate and a greater number of women remaining single past their teen-age years.

"I think this is something of a new, complex syndrome of circumstances we've never had before," said Paul C. Glick, senior demographer in the Census Bureau's population division.

His report noted a change in the role of women. It pointed out the greater number of women working, the higher educational attainments of woman and their increased economic independence from husbands.

The report noted these trends:

The number of marriages dropped by nearly 3 percent in the 12-month period ended last August, the first significant decline since World War II. The divorce rate is at a record of more than 4 per 1,000 persons a year.

The percentage of women remaining single until they are between 20 and 24 years old has climbed from 28 in 1960 to 40 in 1974.

The birth rate is only slightly above the 1973 record low of 15 per 1,000.

Americans are having fewer babies and more of the young and elderly are living alone, accounting for the decline in the average size of households.

Mr. Glick said that the full impact of the trends on people's ability to find companionship and a satisfactory life under new circumstances was not yet clear. "It's going to be different, but not necessarily worse. It will take a while to get used to these changes and that may be what has to be done," Mr. Glick said.

—*The New York Times*, July 6, 1975

Diamonds Are a Girl's Best Friend

I know where I'm going
And I know who's going with me
I know who I love
But the lord knows who'll I'll marry. . .
I have skirts of silk
And shoes of fine green leather
Combs to buckle my hair
And rings for every finger.

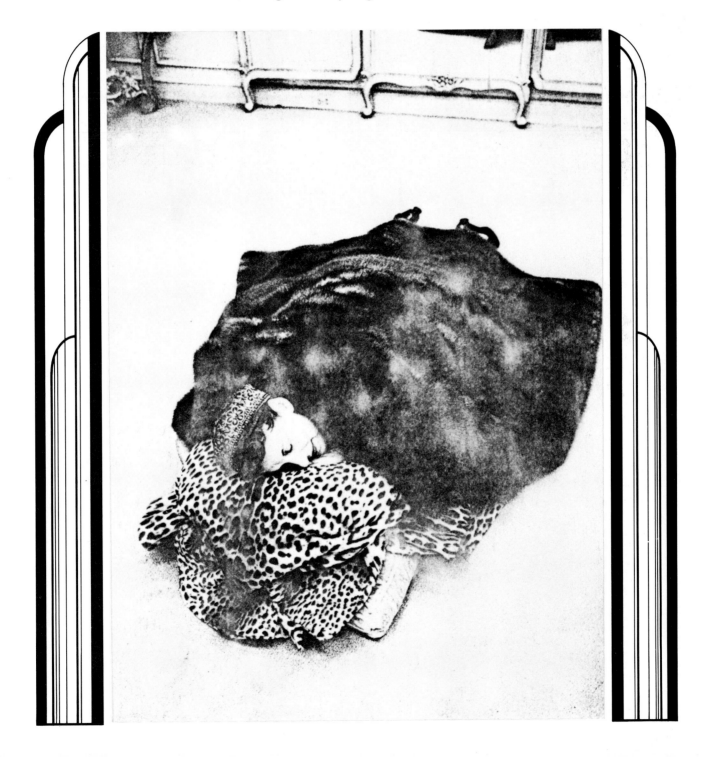

I know where I'm going
And I know who's going with me
I know who I love
But the lord knows who'll I'll marry.

—ballad

FOR women, marriage is the second oldest profession in the world. Like prostitution, the first, it is a business generating income for women. And in these two trades, women most easily earn their daily bread. Harlot with heart of gold, wife with open arms and tidied home, these are hard-working women. Given a choice, marriage is the preferred occupation. So women are expected to marry. Why? Simple: to make babies, to bring dowries, to increase land, wealth, might, power, prestige; to cement communities, tribes, clans, states, empires, nations; to distribute wealth, genes, bloodlines; to ensure the stability and survival of society. They are paid for this work. How?: with food, clothing, shelter, money, life insurance policies, death benefits. And then again: with respectability, status, ease, honor, pleasure, and profit.

Men, in their youth, are prepared for professions, and marriage is not considered as the grand feature in their lives. . . . To rise in the world, and have the liberty of running from pleasure to pleasure . . . [women] must marry advantageously, and to this object their time is sacrificed, and their persons often legally prostituted.

—Mary Wollstonecraft, *A Vindication of the Rights of Woman*, 1792

ILLEGAL prostitution, the woman for hire on the streets; legal prostitution, the wife contracted for sex at home. Whichever she chooses or must choose, woman must work.

Where are you going to, my pretty maid
I'm going a-milking, sir, she said,
Sir, she said, sir, she said,
I'm going a-milking, sir, she said.

May I go with you, my pretty maid?
You're kindly welcome, sir, she said.

Say will you marry me, my pretty maid?
Yes, if you please, kind sir, she said.

What is your father, my pretty maid?
My father's a farmer, sir, she said.

What is your fortune, my pretty maid?
My face is my fortune, sir, she said.

Then I can't marry you, my pretty maid.
Nobody asked you, sir, she said.

—nursery rhyme, 1698

THIS girl can't turn the fortune of a pretty face into cold cash and her father doesn't have enough money to sweeten her looks, so the pretty maid stays single. Yet after the song is sung, how does she survive? How can she afford to live the single life? Sometimes she can't and takes to the streets, that other obvious profession for women. Or she becomes the maiden aunt or the governess, or the nanny, or the seamstress, or the shopgirl, the cleaning woman, the waitress, the barmaid, the go-go dancer.

There have been many ways to lead the single life and, through time, women have devised strategies and skills to live it, some less hard than others.

Don't sing love songs, you'll wake my
    mother,
She's sleeping here, right by my side,
And in her right hand, a silver dagger,
She says that I can't be your bride.

All men are false says my mother,
They'll tell you wicked, lovin' lies,
The very next evening they'll court another,
Leave you alone to pine and sigh.

My daddy is a handsome devil,
He's got a chain five miles long.
And on every link a heart does dangle
For another maid he's loved and wronged.

Go court another tender maiden
And hope that she will be your wife,
For I've been warned and I've decided
To sleep alone all of my life.

—ballad, "Silver Dagger"

The breeding of pedigree dogs and cats for shows and competitions has long been a pursuit as fashionable for women as is the

breeding of race horses for men. Recently, also, various paragraphs have appeared in the Press dealing with such curiosities as silver-fox farms, Angora rabbit farms and skunk farms, which may . . . be run for profit . . .

—Vera Brittain,
Women's Work in Modern England, 1928

But the fact is, through time, women must be able to afford the single life in order to choose it. And then things change when they do choose it.

A somewhat intensive study of the effects upon marriage from woman's access to industry results in the following conclusions: 1. Woman's access to industry lowers the wage scale and makes it harder for men to assume the burdens of matrimony. 2. Industrial opportunity makes women independent of the necessity of marriage. 3. Employment in specialized industry tends to create distaste for housekeeping and so may be a factor in checking marriage. 4. The experience of wage-earning may raise a girl's standard of living so that she will hesitate to marry an ordinary man. 5. Experience in the world brings her in touch with the vice and disease prevalent among men and may cause fear of marriage. 6. Delay of marriage may lead to an irregular sex life, which is very likely to prevent marriage altogether. 7. Women are crowding particularly into professional and other high positions where ambition makes the current against matrimony strongest.

—Calhoun, *The American Family*, 1922

The single woman, with money of her own, can live the single life with pleasure, discrimination, and ease. By choice or chance, the island this independent state rests upon is always money.

"I do so wonder, Miss Woodhouse, that you should not be married, or going to be married! So charming as you are!". . .
"Never mind, Harriet, I shall not be a poor old maid; and it is poverty which makes celibacy contemptible to a generous public!

A single woman, with a very narrow income, must be a ridiculous, disagreeable, old maid!. . . . but a single woman of good fortune, is always respectable. . . ."

—Jane Austen, *Emma*, 1816

A woman says, and we are surprised: "I don't have to get married to live well; of course, I need respectability, but since I can afford to pay for my life—my clothes, my friends, my pleasure, my car, my keys—I can live well. There's no profit motive that would make me marry. I don't know, maybe I won't marry. Anyway, don't talk to me about the pitiful women who can't afford to live alone but have to. I know that the only thing that matters—yes—is that a single woman lives or dies according to the size of her pocketbook."

Everybody knows that—as much as it is anything else—marriage is a business deal. To marry or not, then, is the most serious decision that a woman ever makes. So when a women does not marry, she is making an economic decision; she is setting up a business deal with herself. She holds all the options, packages the product, delivers the goods. But it has always been hard for the majority of women to make as much money as men. So, it is often a very bad investment for a woman to bank on herself. Financial return on her work is always less than a man's.

Look at the European farm workers:

In the twelfth century, the female wage was approximately eighty per cent of male remuneration, by the end of the fourteenth century, it had shrunk to seventy-five per cent and in the fifteenth century it was no more than half. In the sixteenth century . . . women who did the same job as men received only forty per cent of their wages. Examples of this kind abound in the nineteenth century, when women's lot was at its worst. They were then paid fifty to sixty percent less than men for the same work.

—Evelyne Sullerot,
Woman, Society and Change, 1971

The nineteenth century was the very worst time for single women—spinsters—to bet on independent economic survival. For one thing, the only well-paying work for women was marriage and there was suddenly an excess of women. True to the laws of supply and demand, large numbers of women, whose fathers or brothers couldn't keep them, did not marry. They lived dreadful lives.

> The plight of these spinsters was grave indeed. Lacking education, or the possibility of employment in any sphere save that of governess or seamstress, they faced continued penury during their life with the ever-present threat of the work-house and the disgrace of losing class when they became too old to support themselves. By the end of the century the majority of Victorian families were only too well aware of this problem, as the majority of families contained at least one of these 'surplus' women.
>
> —Hannah Gavron, *The Captive Wife*, 1966

To BE a surplus woman—this is the ghost that haunts every single woman who is in the business of herself alone. It stalks her with the threat of ridicule, meanness, loneliness, poverty, degradation.

> There were some others, sort of, but after he split, I knew I'd have to make it on my own. I used to walk along the streets, feeling that everybody was staring at me because I was alone; I'd look into other people's windows and I'd splurge and treat myself to a hamburger in a nice place. I really got crazy about eating—I kept wanting there to be somebody to feed me. And then I'd think about always being alone and never having someone to zip my dress up and then I'd go home and nothing had changed in the room and I'd try to think of someone to call but I ran out of people and then I was really scared about being alone, and having no money.

SINGLE women live this fear. But some singles like Lorelei Lee, heroine of *Gentlemen Prefer Blondes* and professional gold digger, understand the economy of the marketplace. If you don't have money and can't make it, get it: diamonds are a girl's best friend. Cold hard cash, this is the commodity successful single women know they must trade in.

ALL ABOUT EVE

EVE was evicted from the garden of Eden when she plucked her own apple and bit into it. That she shared it with Adam later is another long story. Anyway, as Adam's wife—helpmate, says the Bible—she should have taken her husband window-shopping with her in the first place. Snakes don't bother women who've got a strong man beside them. On her own then and acting alone, Eve was prey to and perpetrator of the dangers of the single life. And this was our first mother.

Her story should have warned generations of women to come about the perils of the single life. But daughters never listen to their mothers. Had Eve, after that brief experience of the single life, looked into the future she would have seen much to alarm her. She would have seen her daughters in:

—singles bars where women drink too much and take home strangers;

—high-rise apartments where country girls turned independent city women lie butchered;

—casting directors's offices where starlets strip for inspection;

—damp convents where it's rumored that at least one nun, "Dame Purnell, a priest's concubine . . . had a child in cherry time";

—Piers Plowman, *The Vision*, c.1390

—London streets where whores lie, filthy, hungry, pox-ridden. "What a deplorable sight is it, to behold Numbers of little Creatures piled up in Heaps upon one another, sleeping in the public streets in the most rigorous Seasons and some of them whose Heads will hardly reach above the Waistband of a Man's Breeches, found to be quick with Child."

—*Satan's Harvest Home: or the Present State of Whorecraft*, 1749

—Schoolrooms in great houses where drab governesses darn socks and fail to teach unruly girls the rudiments of French, Shakespeare, and pettipoint;

—ladies' residences where tired, timid women, "single or sometimes widowed . . . [had] the protection of this comfortable fortress, a place where they could retreat, complete with guards and sign-in sheets and sirens that go off at night if anybody disturbed a barred door."

—Patricia O'Brien, *The Woman Alone*, 1973

SINGLE women live or die according to the size of their pocketbooks. In those historical times when single women could pay their own way, the single life was soundly applauded and the life itself an energetic and powerful one:

. . . what is striking to anyone who lives in a society which upholds marriage as a universal form for women, and which imposes innumerable disabilities on women seeking employment, is the abundance of positions available to single women in the Middle Ages. In thirteenth-century Paris, five of the crafts organized by guilds were defined as monopolies of women, and many of the others employed women in large numbers. . . . Everywhere custom defined as monopolies gainful work as feminine employments, notably brewing and spinning . . . the term "spinster" suggests that spinning, for one, was often an occupation of unmarried women. The failure of medieval records to distinguish between single and married women in the labor market is itself an important piece of information, suggesting that industrial work was not then regarded, as it came to be regarded in the eighteenth and nineteenth centuries, as an activity appropriate only to young women awaiting offers of marriage.

—C. Lasch, "To Marry or to Burn," *Columbia Forum*, 1973

THERE has never been one prescribed way of enjoying or understanding or living the single life. In our day, professions have opened and marriages are more easily broken; we see in the gay divorcée not merely a man hunter or a wronged woman but someone capable of nurturing and, more important, sustaining a life on her own. Yet we fail to remember the past and the opportunities then available to women which have been closed to them ever since.

No institution in Europe has ever won for . . . [the woman] the freedom of development that she enjoyed in the convent in the early days. The modern college for women only feebly reproduces it . . . The lady-abbess . . . was part of the two great social forces of her time, feudalism and the church. Great spiritual rewards and great worldly prizes were alike within her grasp. She was treated as an equal by the men of her class, as is witnessed by letters we still have from popes and emperors to abbesses. She had the stimulus of competition with men in executive capacity, in scholarship and in artistic production, since her work was freely set before the general public; but she was relieved by the circumstances of her environment of the ceaseless competition in common life of woman with woman for the favour of the individual man. In the cloister of the great days, . . . women were judged by each other, as men are everywhere judged by each other, for sterling qualities of head and heart and character.

—Emily James Putnam, *The Lady*, 1910

EVEN more than our age of liberation, medieval times permitted women strategies and skills for leading the single life. Women had vocational training, occupational choices, economic independence, jobs, a life which was respectable. What we think of as the cloistered and still life of the nun was, in fact, busy with activity: girls were sent to convents to learn reading, chanting, singing, writing, painting, spinning, weaving, designing, sewing, embroidery with gold and jewels on silk, church decoration, calligraphy. Out of the busyness of their hands, nuns made the goods for barter, bargain, and empire. We even know of an abbess who minted her own coins, and of others whose economic might was such that they raised their own armies.

Obviously, then, the landed wealth of medieval convents was supported, sustained, and extended by the work of the nuns themselves. Those lilies of the field toiled and spun, weaving the strength of the single life. And at this time, as at no other since, a woman's marital status was often of less importance than her occupation, her trade, her achievements, her single capacity to support her autonomous self.

> I have no complaint,
> Prosperity that
> the golden Muses
> gave me was no
> delusion: dead, I
> won't be forgotten.

—Sappho of Lesbos, Fragment 100

> Somewhere over the rainbow
> Way up high
> There's a land that I've heard of
> Once in a lullaby . . .
> Birds fly over the rainbow
> Why then o why can't I?

—E. Y. Harburg, "Over the Rainbow"

> No, I will go alone.
> I will come back when it's over
> Yes, of course, I love you.
> No, it will not be long.
> Why may you not come with me?—
> You are too much my lover.
> You would put yourself
> Between me and song . . .

—Edna St. Vincent Millay, "The Concert," 1920

WHAT is womansong? Is it loneliness, solitude, celibacy, isolation, selfishness, arrogance, genius? It can be. But it can be as well to know that all by yourself you can be autonomous and grow a little taller.

> Monday, January 26th, 1920
> The day after my birthday; in fact I'm 38, well, I've no doubt I'm a great deal happier than I was at 28; and happier today than I was yesterday having this afternoon arrived at some idea of a new form for a new novel.

—Virginia Woolf, *A Writer's Diary*

The young girl touches her swelling breasts; the mother feels the baby swimming in her belly; the young woman, buying flowers for herself, relishes her own unattachment; the wife lies thinking her own thoughts, in bed beside her sleeping husband; the widow discovers in sorrow the freedoms she didn't know she wanted. These are the private notes of womansong. Such women carry within them the single life. We can mark these moments of celebration, single or unsingle.

And sometimes women give public voice to their song.

> Dearest Mother,—I have tried to be more contented, and I think I have been more so. I have been thinking about my little room, which I suppose I never shall have. I should want to be there all the time, and I should go there and sing and think. . . .

—Louisa May Alcott, *Early Diary Kept at Fruitlands* (at ten years of age), 1843

But in these last three years a great change has come over my life . . . Under the influences of the intense happiness I have enjoyed from thorough moral and intellectual sympathy I have at last found out my true vocation, after which my nature had always been feeling and striving uneasily without finding it. What do you think that vocation is? I pause for you to guess. I have turned out to be an artist—not as you are, with the pencil and the palette, but with words.

—George Eliot, letter, October 18, 1859

The school year was coming to a close, and I got ready to go away on holiday with Sartre. Afterward we would go our separate ways. But now I had resigned myself to the inevitable. I reflected that solitude—in moderate doses—no doubt had its attractions as well as its more obvious virtues. I hoped that it would strengthen me against the temptations I had been dodging for two years now: that of giving up. All my life I will preserve an uneasy memory of this period, of my fear that I might betray my youthful ideal. . . . Today I ask myself how much, in fact, such a risk ever existed. If any man had proved insufficiently self-centered and commonplace to attempt my subjugation, I should have judged him, found him wanting, left him. The only sort of person in whose favor I could ever want to surrender my autonomy would be just the one who did his utmost to prevent any such thing . . .

As I trudged across the rich dark soil of Herault . . . I thought back over the past year with great satisfaction. I hadn't read much, and my own novel was worthless; on the other hand I had worked at my chosen profession without losing heart. . . . I was emerging triumphant from the trials to which I had been subjected: separation and loneliness had not destroyed my peace of mind. I knew that I could now rely on myself.

—Simone de Beauvoir,
The Prime of Life, 1960

Women sing womansong,
sing a song about themselves,
sing a song of solitary woman,
a song of woman single,
a solo song.

The Anatomy of Lust

Wou'd ye have fresh Cheese and Cream?
Julia's Breast can give you them:
And if more; Each *Nipple* cries,
To your *Cream*, here's *Strawberries*.

—Herrick, "Fresh Cheese and Cream," 1648

St. Agatha offering her ablated breasts to God, symbolizing her martyrdom. Painting by Lorenzo Lippi

SKINFLICK

MEN relish women's bodies; they like and know women's flesh better than women do, for a woman seldom savors this moving feast —her anatomy is useful equipment, not erotic meat. Female flesh is food to men: breasts are melons or lemons or apples; skin is cream and marshmallows and brown sugar; buttocks are hot buns and watermelons; and hips are juicy hams.

> Hurriedly she got undressed. I took off my clothes, too. In the moonlight, Bessie looked startlingly white, her breasts huge and round and her buttocks shining like two pale hams . . .
>
> —*True Story*, June, 1975

A GOOD-LOOKING woman is a hot tomato, a Georgia peach waiting to be peeled, a cream puff, a nougat, a chocolate-covered cherry, all ready to be eaten up.

> . . . her navel was carved so deep that it would have held an ounce of nutmeg butter.
>
> —"Tale of Sympathy the Learned," *Arabian Nights*

MUCH of the time women don't know their own lusciousness; much of the time they observe their bodies rather than enjoying those fruits.

> Taught from infancy that beauty is woman's scepter, the mind shapes itself to the body and roaming round its gilt cage, only seeks to adorn its prison.
>
> —Mary Wollstonecraft, *A Vindication of the Rights of Woman*, 1792

When women think of their bodies they think of men looking at them, telling them how they look.

> Brett was damned good-looking. She wore a slipover jersey sweater and a tweed skirt, and her hair was brushed back like a boy's. She started all that. She was built with curves like the hull of a racing yacht, and you missed none of it with that wool jersey.
>
> —Ernest Hemingway, *The Sun also Rises*, 1946

> How fair is thy love, my sister, my spouse!
> How much better is thy love than wine!
> and the smell of thine ointments than all spices!
> Thy lips, O my spouse, drip as the honeycomb;
> honey and milk are under thy tongue;
> and the smell of thy garments is like the smell of Lebanon . . .
>
> Thy plants are an orchard of pomegranates, with pleasant fruits;
> spikenard and saffron;
> calamus and cinnamon;
> myrrh and aloes,
> with all the chief spices. . . .
>
> —Song of Solomon

> Age cannot wither her, nor custom stale
> Her infinite variety; other women cloy
> The appetites they feed, but she makes hungry
> Where most she satisfies. . . .
>
> —Shakespeare, *Antony and Cleopatra*, 1623

> In a minute Jeff was digging me out, throwing back the covers to expose my naked body, admiring it frankly in the light of a small table lamp.
> "You really turn me on, Audrey," he breathed. "I could look at you for hours. Those long legs and brown, nubby nipples. What a centerfold!"
>
> —"Every Night We Had Sex for an Audience," *True Story*, 1975

> Truthfully, if she had not gone further to meet Diamond it was because the heavy haunches slung to so slight a waist prevented her, and because her backside, dimpled with valleys, was so remarkable a benediction that she could not move easily without it trembling like curdled milk in a Badawi's porringer or quince jelly heaped on a plate perfumed with benzoin. . . .
>
> —"Splendid Tales of Prince Diamond," *Arabian Nights*

MEN like women's bodies so much that if there isn't one right beside them to look at, to touch, they will create its image to take along with them wherever they go:

—icons of the Virgin Mary traveled with medieval knights on the Crusades;

—pin-up queens litter the barracks of every campground;

—mechanics decorate their grease pits with calendar art;

—young boys tear centerfolds from girlie magazines to hide in sock drawers and lockers.

The traditional female nude in western art is *not* a tribute to [woman's] own sexuality;

rather, [it is] a function of the sexuality of the owner-spectator [male] . . .

—Linda Nochlin, "The Female Nude
in 19th Century Art,"
Edited by Thomas Hess and E. C. Baker,
Art and Sexual Politics, 1973

ALTHOUGH men always look at women, they rarely see the whole woman inside and out. Anatomy for them is dissection: they are leg men, tit men, ass men. Men possess women's bodies; they appropriate them; they own them in flesh, fantasy, photo, and artifact.

Lucy was not like other lasses,
From twelve her breasts swell'd in a trice,
First they were like two cupping-glasses,
Then like two peaches made of ice.

—John Hall Stevenson, *Crazy Tales*, 1894

PINNED UP

The girl is looking at the new dress which transfigures her . . . she leans over very close to look at the humid eyes, the humid mouth, the moisture and luminousness brought about by the change of dress. . . . Every girl of fifteen has put the same question to the mirror: "Am I beautiful?" . . . She is watching for an expression which will betray the spirit. You can never catch the face alive, laughing or loving. At sixteen she is looking at the mirror with her hair up for the first time. There is always the question. The mirror is not going to answer it. She will have to look for the answer in the eyes and faces of the boys who dance with her, men later, and above all the painters.

—Anaïs Nin, *Diary*, Volume II

WOMEN wonder about their own erotic chemistry, how their bodies cast sexual spells. Bemused, a woman stands before the mirror; what does her body look like, what should it look like? When other people see her body, how does it appear to them? What is it they see?

It is a commonplace observation that women are forever trying to straighten their hair if it is curly and curl it if it is straight, bind their breasts if they are large and pad them if they are small. . . . Not all these measures are dictated by the phantom of fashion. They all reflect dissatisfaction with the body as it is, and an insistent desire that it be otherwise, not natural but controlled, fabricated. Many of the devices adopted by women are not cosmetic or ornamental, but disguise of the actual, arising from fear and distaste. . . .

—Germaine Greer
The Female Eunuch, 1970

HOWEVER men advertise women's anatomy, women know that their flesh serves other purposes besides sex. Breasts which titillate men are also for suckling infants and comforting children. Stomachs are the cushion of love, but the seat, too, of cramps, kicks, spasms, and malignant tumors.

Clean of the body's hair,
I lie smooth from breast to leg.
All that was special, all that was rare
is common here. Fact: death too is in the
 egg.
Fact: the body is dumb, the body is meat.
And tomorrow the O.R. Only the summer
 was sweet.

—Anne Sexton, "The Operation," 1962

Ever since you last saw me inclined to faint, I have felt some gentle twitches, which make me begin to think that I am nourishing a creature who will soon be sensible of my care. . . . Yesterday—do not smile— finding that I had hurt myself by lifting precipitately a large log of wood, I sat down in agony, till I felt those said twitches again. . . .

—Mary Wollstonecraft,
letter to Imlay, 1794

And I curled up at the feet of Sido, my head at her knees. The three o'clock sunlight closed my eyelids and the to-and-fro movement of the comb made me drowsy. In the depths of a rattan armchair slept a pregnant cat. . . . Blissful, the mongrel bitch suckled her mongrel pups. . . . No half-grown males anywhere, no sign of a man. Mothers. Children still ignorant of their sex. The deep peace of a harem, under the nests of May and the wisteria shot with sunlight. I was no longer linked with the real world, except by the purring of the cat, the clear ringing of a nearby anvil, and the hands of my mother at the back of my neck, deftly braiding my hair. . . .

—Colette, *Earthly Paradise*, 1966

TO MEN, women's bodies are for creature comforts. To women, their bodies are for the comforts of other creatures: men, children, and the riddles of nature.

From puberty to menopause woman is the theater of a play that unfolds within her and in which she is not personally concerned.

—Simone de Beauvoir,
The Second Sex, 1949

YET women do experience the comforts and discomforts of other creatures in their bodies very personally.

> After my dear child's death, I fell into a great and long-continued weakness by the swelling of my milk, his having sucked last, in his pain, of the left breast, had hurt the nipple, causing it to gangrene and extreme pained with the torment of it, made me fall into a fever, which together with excessive pains in my head and teeth, upon much grief from the unhandsome proud carriage of those I took to be a comfort in my distress, proved the greatest corrosive in my sick and weak condition.

> —Alice Thornton, *Autobiography*, 1667

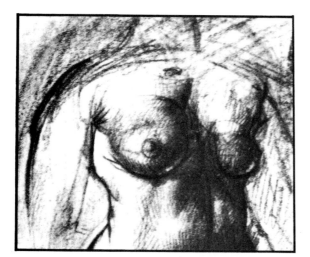

PERSONAL or impersonal, the female body is communal property. Something is always coming into it or going out of it, or going out or coming in: blood, babies, sperm, good and bad secretions, tampons, douches, pessaries, doctor's hands (his instruments, too), or someone's fondling it, nuzzling it, stroking, petting, pinching, poking, tugging, striking, kicking. And these same bodies are to suckle, comfort, cushion, and excite. When forced to be alone with her body before the mirror, during menstruation and menopause, after the door closes on a lover—woman often inhabits an alien home. Through most of her life, in fact, she is a stranger in a strange land.

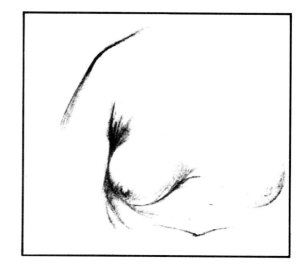

I watch my daughter. From morning to night her body is her home. She lives in it and with it. When she runs around the kitchen she uses all of herself . . . When she rubs her crotch, there is no awkwardness, no feeling that what she is doing is wrong. She knows when she wants to be touched and when she wants to be left alone . . . It's beautiful to be with her. I sometimes feel she is more of a model for me than I am for her! Occasionally I feel jealous of the ease with which she lives inside her skin. I want to be a child again! It's so hard to get back that sense of body as home.

> —"Sexual Feelings,"
> *Our Bodies, Ourselves*, 1971

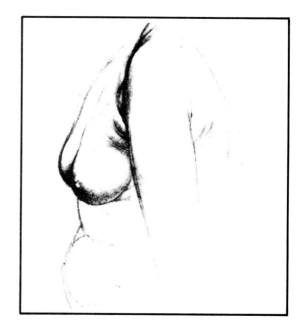

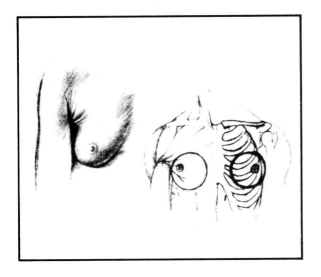

She didn't even know she had a neck until Jude remarked on it, or that her smile was anything but the spreading of her lips until he saw it as a small miracle.

—Toni Morrison, *Sula*, 1973

BUT the same music and words and pictures freeze the image of that beauty, immortalize it, and make adored woman a captive of her self.

THE geography of the human female body, its anatomy, changes all the time, every month. A little girl has a flat chest, and then breasts. She has a flat stomach and then it rounds and then, perhaps it flattens again. A woman can bear children—and then she cannot. The destiny of woman's anatomy is change. Woman often knows how she is erotic only when a man tells her so; when he celebrates her in story and song, but especially in picture and—heaven help her!—in photographs.

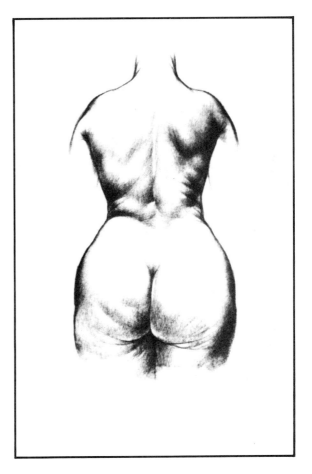

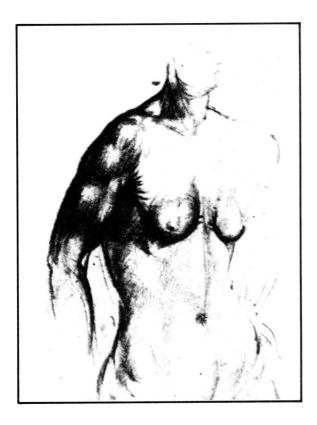

WHATEVER men see, for women the photograph is also an X-ray. She knows that beneath the picture of gorgeous flesh lives the reality of tissue, bone, muscle, blood.

Sometimes she dismisses the photograph, submits to the X-ray which shows those imperfections, the pimples, the ragged hairline, the crooked nose, the fat belly, the veined calves, and feels that the photograph lies. And that men—or women—who are wooing her, describing her special beauty, tell lies, too.

The Anatomy of Lust / 125

"I can't go to that party. I'm fat and ugly. My stockings have a rip in them—and if I don't wear the blue ones, then I can't wear this dress. If I can't wear this dress, then I've got nothing to wear. I can't stand myself."

"Honey, you look fine."

AT OTHER times, woman worships the photograph because she, too, loves what she sees.

Yes, she was indeed a beautiful woman, she decided, catching sight of herself in a long mirror as she came out of the cloak-room at Buckingham Palace. She was alone in the passage. . . . She could take stock of herself in the mirror without any consciousness of men watching her. . . . So she loitered, having come out of the cloak-room only to face an unexpected mirror that returned to her, full-length, the image of the complete woman. . . . Here, in the long mirror, she saw herself not only as a kit-cat, but full-length: oyster satin flowing out at her feet, pearls vanishing into the valley between her breasts, pearls looped round her wrists, a rosy scarf tossed round her shoulders. . . . Satisfied by the image that the mirror returned to her, she gave herself a little smile.

—Vita Sackville-West,
The Edwardians, 1930

Do WOMEN ever put the two together—pulchritude and protoplasm, flawed flesh and the unique contours that live there? Somewhere, in the kaleidoscope of others' vision of her, is one lucid image. How does she find it? Through her own eyes, which are the truest lens. When, like the camera, woman's eye focuses with detachment, without sexual desire or design, it can capture the idiosyncrasies of blood, flesh, skin, hair, and bone. And woman suddenly sees that no matter who the current pin-up queen may be, she, too, possesses the beauty of the human form.

All women fear time and change, for woman's anatomy can only live to betray her. And make men, in their turn, betray her as well.

DISSECTED

Tonight I've watched
the moon and then
The Pleiades
go down

The night is now
half-gone; youth
goes; I am
in bed alone—

—Sappho of Lesbos, Fragment 64

WHY does a wise woman live in fear of the younger woman in whose skin beauty is still deep? For the younger woman is herself in fear; she, too, is haunted by the specter of on-coming age, that beast who will never be kissed and turned miraculously young again.

Sundry names given to the Sexual Organs of Women

El hacene (the beautiful)—this is the vulva which is white, plump, in form vaunted like a dome, firm, and without any de-formity. You cannot take your eyes off it, and to look at it changes a feeble erection into a strong one.

El gueunfond (the hedgehog)—the vulva of the old, decrepit woman, dried up with age and with bristly hair.

—*The Perfumed Garden of Shaykh Nefzawi,* fourteenth century

WOMEN often know themselves as erotic ob-jects only by reflecting on their reflection in men's eyes. But while men relish women's flesh, they have also been known to loathe and fear women's bodies.

Another version of the theme appears in the mythology of the Toba Indians of the Gran Chaco of South America. The chief characters in this story are Big Fox, a bawdy trickster, and Hawk. Both went hunting with a group of other beings who were a blend of animal and man. At this time men had no women. Hawk had the good fortune to encounter some women climbing down from the sky on ropes. Hawk cleverly cut

the ropes, causing' the women to fall down to earth. There were enough to provide all the men with mates. Hawk, however, had noticed that the women were provided with toothed vaginas and advised caution. Fox being sexually greedy could not wait and as soon as he started to make love to his woman she cut off his penis and testicles with her vagina. Fox died of his wound. A little later rain fell upon him which brought him to life. He made a new penis of wood and testicles from two black fruits. Then he went back and copulated with his wife. She tried her best to bite off his penis but only succeeded in denting it The next day Hawk picked up a stone and broke off all the teeth in the women's vaginas except one which became the clitoris. He said, "Now wait. Tomorrow your wives will be well again and you may copulate with them."

—H. R. Hays, myth of Toba Indians of the Gran Chaco of South America, *Dangerous Sex,* 1964

EVEN at their best, men's eyes give back imperfect impressions of women: some men think that the women they love are eternally young, or beautiful, or sexy, or smart. Some men, with crueler eyes, watch as tits become dugs, asses become cans, and one chin folds into many. A stitch around the line cannot save time. However she disfigures her body to arrest time's scaring, woman cannot change the fact of her aging.

A woman is usually more narcissistic in love than a man; her narcissism is directed at her body as a whole. She has a delightful awareness of her body as something desirable, and this awareness comes to her through her partner's caresses and his gaze. If he goes on desiring her she easily puts up with her body's ageing. But at the first sign of coolness she feels her ugliness in all its horror, she is disgusted with her image and cannot bear to expose her poor person to others. This lack of assurance strengthens her fear of other people's opinions: she knows how censorious they are towards old women who do not play their proper role of serene and passion-free grandmothers.

—Simone de Beauvoir,
The Second Sex, 1949

IF woman relies only upon men's images of her, then the youthful flesh she yearns still to live in—through the celebration, mirrors, and icons of men—becomes a dry dead husk around her. She's pinned up and can't remove the pins. If women live in bodies borrowed from men, then when men discard these bodies—when these bodies no longer hold interest for men—women are bankrupt. Completely possessed by man for her youthful succulence, aging woman is dispossessed.

AWAKENED

Neither history nor literaure has left us any worthwhile evidence on the sexuality of old women. It is an even more strictly forbidden subject than the sexuality of old men.

—Simone de Beauvoir,
The Coming of Age, 1972

OLD AGE brings something new to women: choice. Standing before the mirror, aged women sees her own reflection. Observing the startling image she sees, she can wince, she can weep, or she can win her own world.

Perhaps the next generation will look deeper into this matter, and find that contempt is put on . . . old women . . . merely because they do not use the elixir which will keep the soul always young. No one thinks of Michael Angelo's Persian Sibyl, or St. Theresa, or Tasso's Leonora, or the Greek Electra as [an old woman] though all had reached the period of life's course appointed to take that degree.

—Margaret Fuller, *The Great Lawsuit. Man Versus Man. Woman Versus Women.* 1843

ALTHOUGH woman winces before the mirror, she continues the struggle to arrest time.

I wish I could have a face-lift
Not for anybody else but for me.
Or it might be for my husband (Who loves me
But thinks I still look as I used to be) . . .

It's out of delicacy that I write to you in rhyme,
Would it be unreasonable . . . would it be out of place . . .
If I asked you to take a stitch in my face?

—Enid Bagnold, *Autobiography*, 1969

'Sit down, and tell me what you want to know.'
'Did you take off my ears?'
'No, I just lifted them a little and tucked everything in behind.'
'How much skin did you take off?'
'Enough to cover a handbag.'

—Bagnold, *Autobiography*, 1969

"But back to the plastic surgery. People wonder if having an operation can change a person's self-image. It absolutely has changed mine. I have more pride. I dress better. I take more pains with my clothing. It never bothered me on stage to look awful, it was part of the act. It was in my personal life that it bothered me. Now I'm more likely to get all fixed up. I feel so much better about myself. I used to slop around—because I didn't look that good if I did. HaHAA!"

Her friends tried to dissuade her from having surgery. "You'll ruin your career," they said.

"But I looked in the mirror and didn't like what I saw. So I did it anyway." She jokes that in a school production of Cinderella she played *both* ugly sisters.

It couldn't happen now. Not to this Cinderella of the Geritol set.

—Mary Beth Moster,
"Baby you're Beautiful!:
Phyllis Diller on Face-Lifts," *Girl Talk*, 1975

A FACE-LIFT often isn't enough—a young lover must be found.
    Older woman says:

I can assure you that wrinkles, or a small stoop in the shoulders, nay grey hair itself, is no objection to the making of new conquests. I know you cannot easily figure to yourself a young fellow of five-and-twenty ogling my Lady Suff—with passion, or pressing to lead the Countess of O—d from an opera. But such are the sights I see every day, and I don't perceive any body surprised at them but myself. A woman, till five-and-thirty, is only looked upon as a raw girl, and can possibly make no noise in the world till about forty. I don't know what your ladyship may think of this matter; but 'tis a considerable comfort to me, to know there is upon earth such a paradise for old women...

—Lady Mary Wortley Montagu, *Letter*,
Vienna, September 20, 1716

"Balzac," he continues, pressing on the table in a way that stays my brush, "was younger than me when he took a married woman with a grown-up family about her as his first love. She was his friend, adviser, companion, mother and mistress to him. He never once looked at a younger woman, to whom he had access in every stage of dress and undress in the theatre world. He found

them self-centred and depthless whereas he found simply everything in his woman of forty-five. They remained faithful and together for fifteen years. He wrote about her, "There is nothing to compare with the first love of a man with the last love of a woman." He pours the French [wine] again clumsily into his glass and pours it with equal clumsiness down his throat. Then he raises it, empty. "My dear," he whispers, "to you."

—Sylvia Ashton-Warner, *Spinster*, 1958

I prefer a young man for coition and him
    only
He is full of courage—he is my sole ambition.
His member is . . . richly proportioned in all
    its dimensions;
It has a head like to a brazier.
Enormous, and none like it in creation;
Strong it is and hard, with the head rounded
    off.
It is always ready for action and does not
    die down;
It never sleeps, owing to the violence of its
    love.

—"Concerning Women who Deserve to Be
    Praised,"
The Perfumed Garden, fourteenth century

BEFORE the mirror, however, many women weep.

The woman who has grown old
And knows desire must die,
Yet turns to love again,
Hears the crows' cry.

She is a stem long hardened.
A weed that no scythe mows.
The heart's laughter will be to her
The crying of the crows.

Who slide in the air with same voice
Over what yields not, and what yields,
Alike in spring, and when there is only bitter
Winter-burning in the fields.

—Louise Bogan, "The Crows," 1954

That evening, while preparing for bed, Mrs. Bridge suddenly paused with the fingertips

of one hand just touching her cheek. She was seated before her dressing table in her robe and slippers and had begun spreading cold cream on her face. The touch of the cream, the unexpectedness of it—for she had been thinking deeply about how to occupy tomorrow—the swift cool touch demoralized her so completely that she almost screamed.

She continued spreading the cream over her features, steadily observing herself in the mirror, and wondered who she was and how she happened to be at the dressing table, and who the man was who sat on the edge of the bed taking off his shoes. She considered her fingers, which dipped into the jar of their own accord. Rapidly, soundlessly, she was disappearing into white, sweetly scented anonymity. Gratified by this she smiled, and perceived a few seconds later that beneath the mask she was not smiling. All the same, being committed, there was nothing to do but proceed.

—Evan Connell, *Mrs. Bridge*, 1958

Do WE ALL vanish beneath the vanishing cream? No. A handsome young prince's kiss brought Sleeping Beauty back to youth and passion after a hundred years of sleep and silence. This is the fable. In real time, there is no prince to kiss away a woman's years, no charm to still the passing of time. For all women age dispels that magic which youth and beauty cast. But age itself can awaken and enhance the lust for life. For some women the body becomes—for the first time—a contented home.

. . . you only begin to discover the difference between what you really are, your real self, and your appearance, when you get a bit older. . . . A whole dimension of life suddenly slides away and you realize that what in fact you've been using to get attention has been what you look like. . . . It's a biological thing. It's totally and absolutely impersonal. It has nothing to do with you. It really is a most salutary and fascinating

experience to go through, shedding it all. Growing old is really extraordinarily interesting.

—Doris Lessing (Josephine Hendin, "Doris Lessing: The Phoenix Midst Her Fires," *Harper's*, July 1973)

Before I left the Clinic I asked him if I should need to have the facial operation done again.

"Not for ten years," he said rather strangely, "and then you won't want it." Well, it's ten years and it's true I don't want it: I care too little how I look.

—Bagnold, *Autobiography*, 1969

FOR some few women, when the body has ceased its magnetic pull, when there is no more melancholy in anatomy, the flesh suddenly frees the spirit. And the spirit awakens and germinates and grows.

Menopause itself is no longer a period to fear and wonder about. It is simply a time when menstruation stops and you can no longer become pregnant. As far as I could tell, from interviewing all the women around, this was a redeeming feature for all but one person, who had a hysterectomy at thirty-three. Of course, it coincides with the aging process, and as much as we look forward to growing older, it is quite an adjustment to accept yourself with the wrinkles, the sagging, and the aches and pains that may follow. In my case, however, I really feel better. . . . I have come to terms with me, though, and that's the most important adjustment. I like what I'm doing. I feel worthwhile; my marriage is better than during the period when my children were all at home. I am looking forward to perfecting some more skills, reading so many books I've never had time for, and sharing thoughts and feelings with more people . . . Now, after all these years, I realize that I'm just another human being.

—"Menopause," *Our Bodies/Ourselves*, 1971

Any one who knows from experience what bodily infirmity is—how it spoils life even for those who have no other trouble—gets a little impatient of healthy complainants, strong enough for extra work and ignorant of indigestion. I at least should be inclined to scold the discontented young people, who tell me in one breath that they never have anything the matter with them, and that life is not worth having—if I did not remember my own young discontent. It is remarkable to me that I have entirely lost my personal melancholy. I often, of course, have melancholy thoughts about the destinies of my fellow-creatures, but I am never in that *mood* of sadness which used to be my frequent visitant even in the midst of external happiness. And this, notwithstanding a very vivid sense that life is declining and death close at hand . . .

—George Eliot, *Letter*, November 22, 1876

Network, Patchwork, Good Work

AFGHAN

noun: a blanket or shawl of colored wool, knitted or crocheted in strips or squares which are joined by sewing or crocheting.

WOMEN don't know how much they know, or how they come to know what they know. Yet there is so much that they know how to do, so much wisdom that they share. And for this they rely on *womantalk*.

". . . the wear and tear of those machines is something terrible, you can put things in and they come out in ribbons, now I can keep things for years, I had some pillowcases, embroidered ones, I'd washed them by hand in pure soap for ten years, and then my sister-in-law persuades me to put them in her machine, and when I get them out they're all frayed down the edges. It just shows you, doesn't it?"

"It certainly does," said Woman C, "I think it must be all that rubbing and scrubbing that does it, when you do it by hand you rub too hard, you know, no wonder things don't last, you can't expect them to last."

Woman A, unable to bear her exclusion any longer, suddenly yelled to both of them, "Do yours eat spinach? You wouldn't believe the trouble I've had getting mine to eat spinach, and my husband, he loves it, but I can't go buying it just for him, can I?"

—Margaret Drabble, *The Millstone*, 1965

I stand here ironing, and what you asked me moves tormented back and forth with the iron.

"I wish you would manage the time to come in and talk with me about your daughter. I'm sure you can help me understand her . . ."

—Tillie Olsen, "I Stand Here Ironing," 1954

"Well, sister, you're late; what's the matter?" said Mrs. Glegg, rather sharply, as they shook hands.

Mrs. Pullet sat down—lifting up her

mantle carefully behind, before she answered,—

"She's gone". . . .

"Died the day before yesterday," continued Mrs. Pullet; "an' her legs were as thick as my body," she added. . . . "They'd tapped her no end o' times and the water—they say you might ha' swum in it, if you liked."

"Well, Sophy, it's a mercy she's gone, then, whoever she may be," said Mrs. Glegg. ". . . but I can't think who you're talking of, for my part."

—George Eliot, *Mill on the Floss*, 1860

"Your sister's married, ain't she?"

"That don't make her a woman. Anyway, Mama keeps telling her it's time for her to start acting like a woman. She might've had it in her, but that don't make her no woman. . . ."

When, I first started bleeding, I tried to get back at her. I said, "You said it would be red. It looks like chocolate." "It'll get red," she told me, and it did.

—Gayle Jones, *Corregidora*, 1975

"He doesn't love me, Mother," said Dottie in a low voice. "I just excite him sexually. He told me so." Mrs. Renfrew closed her eyes for an instant. . . . "So he *was* your lover." There had only been one night it seemed. . . . "But you hardly knew him," said Mrs. Renfrew. "Dick's a fast worker," replied Dottie with a twinkle and a cough. . . . "Was it a very painful experience? Did you bleed a great deal, dear?" "No," said Dottie, "It wasn't painful that way. Actually, it was terribly thrilling and passionate. But afterward. . . . He made me . . . go to a doctor and get a contraceptive, one of those diaphragm things you were talking about". . . . "Men are strange," said Mrs. Renfrew.

—Mary McCarthy, *The Group*, 1954

I imagine the following sculpture as utterly beautiful: a pregnant woman chiseled out of stone. Carved only down to the knees so that she looks the way Lise said she did the time she was pregnant with Maria: "As if I am rooted to the ground." The immobility, restraint, introspection. The arms and hands dangling heavily, the head lowered, all attention directed inward. And the whole thing in heavy, heavy stone. Title: Pregnancy.

—Käthe Kollwitz,
Journal, September 1, 1911

What I have to say is really distinct from the artist and art. *It is the woman who has to speak.* And it is not only the woman Anaïs who has to speak, but I who have to speak for many women.

—Anaïs Nin, *Diary*, 1966

One thing I just couldn't bring myself to do was breastfeed the babies, although I loved them. I've got a thing about it, that it sort of nauseates me in a way: I had a long talk with the doctor about it. It worried me that I should breastfeed for the children's sake, partly because my mother-in-law breastfed six and she said I was denying them their birthright. My mother was quite impartial really: although she breastfed both of us, she'd never even mention the subject. I don't know what it is, because I think of myself as being feminine, but I just couldn't bring myself to do that. . . . The girl downstairs had a baby a couple of months ago, and she just cries and cries, and I'm sure she's hungry because she's breastfed. . . .

—"Margaret Nicholson,"
in Ann Oakley, *Woman's Work*, 1975

Christ, what are patterns for?

—Amy Lowell, "Patterns," 1915

Sometimes woman's talk *is* woman's work. Talking, purring, chastising, advising, women join together and sew and crochet and embroider and mend and patch and stitch the seams of daily life. Womantalk is this crazy quilt, this hodgepodge, this colored afghan, embracing the community which is woman's own.

And where do women learn what they know and what they know how to do? Not in libraries, universities, synagogues, stock exchanges, although women learn things there too. Women learn woman's work within the community of women.

Friday, Oct. 7 . . . Mary goes to bed at half-past 8; Shelley sits up with Jane. Talk of oppression and reform, of cutting squares of skin from the soldiers' backs. Jane states her conception of the subterranean community of women . . .

—Percy Bysshe Shelley, *Journal*, 1814

"Don't worry," said the woman in the next bed, giving Martha an amused look. "You can do anything to a baby" . . . Martha therefore lay back and refused to worry. She had accepted this woman as a guide. . . . Martha found the tolerant matron—she was perhaps thirty—frightening because she had three children and was so satisfied to be a maternal housewife, but at the same time inexpressibly comforting. Through her, Martha was accepted into this community of women . . .

—Doris Lessing, *A Proper Marriage*, 1954

The community of women—it's not on any map, not in any book, not in any lecture hall. Glance at any village square: where are the women? what are they doing? Talking. Working. See them together, at the base of monuments, museum rooms, cathedrals—parks, outside the schools, before the stalls of the marketplace, in bedrooms, kitchens, bathrooms, beauty parlors, classrooms, typing pools, nursing stations, laboratories, switchboards, sweatshops, revival meetings, backstages, consciousness-raising groups—wherever they are, whatever they do, women assemble, women labor, women design the fabric of their communal life. What we think of as women's chirping, chattering, muttering, female intuition or feminine instinct, girltalk, bitchery or ball-breaking, old wives' tales is, in fact, woman's wisdom, the subterranean lore of generic life. Women know that womantalk is often woman's work. Womantalk unearths the encrusted nuggets of woman's lore.

Gossip: . . . and did you know that when she was five months pregnant she was still sleeping with her husband's partner?

News: . . . so she went away to college but it broke her father's heart . . .

Trade: . . . so when I see you at Marjorie's, Wednesday night, for bridge, I'll bring the money for you but don't do what Ellen did to me last week when I gave her the money for the sweater and she . . .

Lemon Squeeze: . . . now, Sally, you've given me advice all my life and I'd just like to tell you, for your own good, that you really are too stuck-up . . .

Advice: . . . If you want the house when Mother dies, you get her to put it in writing in the will, but don't say I told you to . . .

Instruction: It was exactly the same when I was nursing Julie—when she cried everybody insisted she was hungry, but you know that the baby's getting milk and if you want to let him stay there and suck, do it.

History: You remember that time when Granddaddy used to show up with the ten suitcases and he always got that same poor cabdriver and I'd send Daddy out—zip—with a quarter for the man because Granddaddy didn't believe in tipping and . . .

Revelation: I never realized it before—there I was sitting in the restaurant alone, eating by myself, before I went back to the hotel and I didn't mind it, actually, I enjoyed it. I was so glad I hadn't just settled for a sandwich in the cafeteria.

Strategy: How long is it since you've done a striptease for him?

Crusade: Men accomplish; it's all set up for them, there's no question about that. And you've accomplished a lot of things too and now probably it's your turn. You can't compare yourself with a man. Men and women are just different, which doesn't mean it's bad.

Sorrow: I don't think I'm leaving him because it's easier to get divorced now. I'm doing it because I know I have to.

Lore: Times were different then and it's good for you to know how other women did it. Aunt Ella worked very hard; she used to stand at the sink with a washboard and scrub with Felsnaptha soap. She'd stand and work in her husband's high-button shoes to ease the pain of standing so long. Then there was the cooking, the cleaning, the ironing—we all wore starched dresses and pinafores over them—the marketing, not supermarketing, but going to the grocer, the butcher, the greengrocer. Aunt Ella would only stop when my mother came with her babies and sit down for a cup of tea. You should remember what a wonderful woman she was . . .

PIECEWORK

noun: work done by the piece and paid for at a standard rate for each unit produced.

Life is a toil and love is a trouble,/ beauty
   will fade and riches will flee/ Pleasures
   they dwindle and prices they double,/
   and nothing is as I would wish it to be.
There's too much of worriment goes to a
   bonnet
There's too much of ironing goes to a shirt.
There's nothing that pays for the time you
   waste on it,
There's nothing that lasts us but trouble and
   dirt.
It's sweeping at six and it's dusting at seven,
It's victuals at eight and it's dishes at nine.
It's potting and panning from ten to eleven
We scarce break our fast till we plan how to
   dine.

—"The Housewife's Lament," from the diary
   of Mrs. Sara A. Price, Ottawa, Illinois,
   nineteenth century

MUCH of woman's time is occupied with piece-work—pieces of work which do not easily fit together. Think of housework, the work that is never done. And how can it be? The worker's eye and hand and mind continually chafes at the sight and touch and sound and smell of things not done, overdone, to be done, and underdone:

—the closet that isn't cleaned, and if it is, it won't be for long;

—the medicine cabinet that hoards pills which, six years from now, can still kill;

—the teenager's room where objects have turned to slime, socks into fossils, and heaps of clothes grow parasites;

—the photography album that sleeps in a cardboard box, year after year, while pictures accumulate around it;

—the stacks of thank-you notes or Christmas cards annoying you until they're done —or nearly done;

—the name tapes; missing socks; leftover roast beef; cracked buttons; chipped teapot tops or cups or saucers; empty toilet paper rolls; carpet stains; and . . .

Eat, eliminate, prepare food, clean up, shop, throw out the garbage, a routine clear as a geometric form, a linear pattern that seems almost graceful in its simplicity. Despite computers and digit telphone numbers, nuclear fission, my life hardly differs from that of an Indian squaw settled in a tepee on the same Manhattan land centuries ago. Pick, clean, prepare, throw out, dig a hole, bury the waste—she was my sister. She would understand why there should be one day of total fast each week.

—Anne Roiphe, *Up the Sandbox*, 1970

I chanced to ask Laura where Mr. J. was to dress. Why says she in the shower bathroom. I told her I'd passed it ¼ an hour ago and saw it full of dirty cloathes for the wash. She begged I would go and look at it and sure enough its furniture consisted of 4 dirty cloathes bags all overflowing, the shower bath full of ditto—a band box of old shoes —and a heap of cast off cloaks of the maids. On investigating further I found every drawer in the Jebb's bedroom crammed with odds and ends of Laura's, . . . so I screeched till I got everybody I could collect and piled all their aprons with the contents which were haycocked in Laura's room for the present. Where the dirty things went I never asked.

—Marianne Thornton,
A Domestic Biography, 1797–1887

Oh dear, says Lady Fritterfame, . . . I was induced, from mere motives of charity, to take into my house a daughter of Colonel Howitzer, who was killed in America. I only expected her to make up my millenery and dresses, clean my laces, write my cards, answer my letters of business, superintend my house accounts, and embroider a court dress. . . . For this I permitted her to dine with me when I had *no* company, or nobody I *cared for*, and gave her *twenty pounds* a year; she had the impertinence, because I ordered her to clean and feed my birds, and

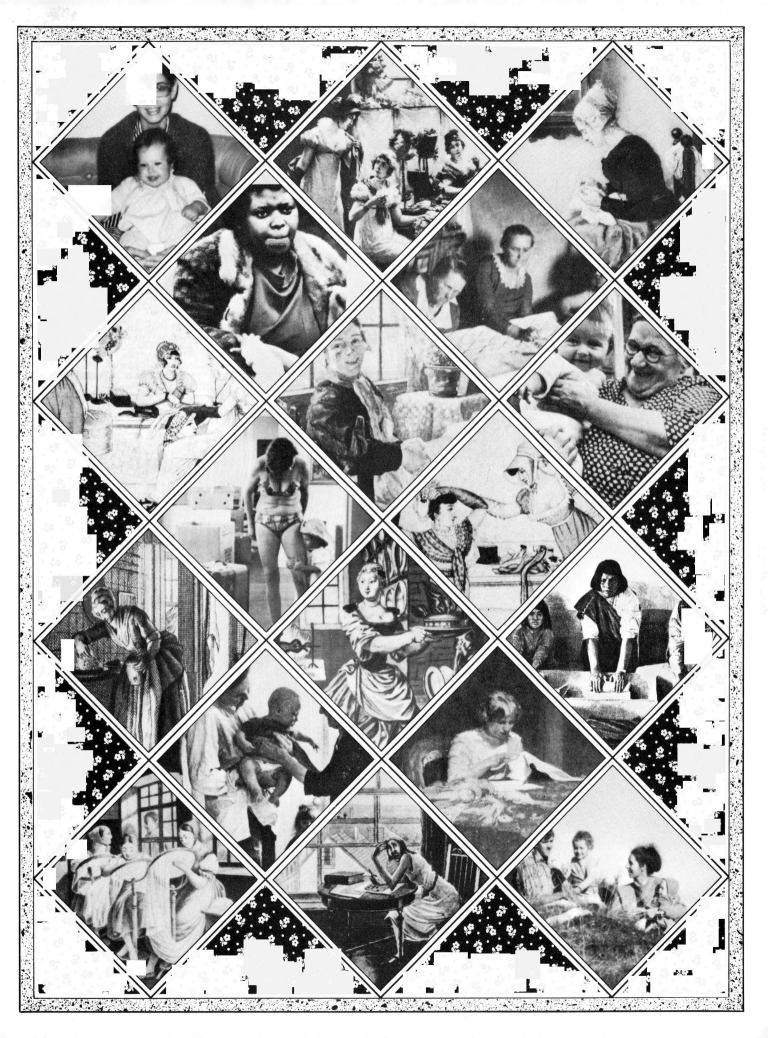

to wash and comb poor dear little Fidelle, to tell me that she did the work of all the servants in my house, without their *wages*; and that, tho' she had condescended to wait upon me, she certainly should not think it equally necessary, to *attend* my birds and beasts.

—Mary Ann Hanway,
Ellinor: Or, the World as It Is, 1798

I worked in the cowshed, as did my husband. I had a small child and often I worked on Shabbat, so I always had a headache about where my child was (on Saturday morning the children's houses were closed). My child hated the cowshed, so he never came there, but other children did. When my turn came to work in the cowshed in the evening shift, I wasn't able to put him to bed for two or three months.

—Lionel Tiger and Joseph Shepher,
a kibbutz woman quoted in
Women in the Kibbutz, 1975

And now we bought that country house, the city that I live in. I wonder what the medieval ladies did, as they travelled between their several castles, about the forgotten engagement-book, the novel left by the bedside, the sleeping pills. [My husband] Roderick at once duplicated everything. I never could. . . . So from the buying of this second house we entertained both ends. Both ends of that journey up and down—Mondays and Fridays in my car. I drove the maids; the maids gave notice; the flowers . . . died in the vases. And inserted in this hurrying, stumbling, list-making life I wrote, and always wrote, those rigid hours. It had the effect that, like Pavlov's dogs, I salivated as I laid my hand on my door (at either end). Gone were the housemaids' troubles as I shut it. Once inside I tried not to dust, not to rearrange the books. All writers know this trembling delay, the fear of the impact with the want of talent.

—Enid Bagnold, *Autobiography*, 1969

Margaret: You know, it's not difficult for me, because I'm very blessed and very lucky . . . because I have a big staff who are willing to work for me . . . and I think they're willing

to help. And my children are beautiful. . . . They have an experimental school going on in the basement and I'm going to be working in the home. I'm going to be doing photographs and stories, and just taking a few hours here, and a few hours there . . .
Interviewer: Is that your message, that freedom is the only solution?
Margaret: No, my message is, like, women have to stop bitching and start getting together and using their time to work side by side with the men and get to the problems of the women and the children. . . .
Interviewer: Where are you going from here? . . .
Margaret: Well, just try to look after the boys and my husband and do just a little bit of putting together, and perhaps a small, very small article which I hope will be judged . . . not because it was done by the wife of the Prime Minister, but . . .

—Margaret Trudeau on herself:
"I Just Want to Work,"
Toronto Star, February 13, 1976

Tuesday morning, January 21st, 1936 Depressed all morning. The trouble is that kind of depression can only be fought with those wells of resource of yourself those things in you that are essentially and most intensely you. . . . And I cannot even think about them now. There is not time, no space, no quiet. Nothing to encourage me, and everything seems to say to me: Give it up; you can never—and you know it—write anything more than a travelogue. . . . I did not feel like the 'wise, gentle, and firm Mother' today! I was very irritable and then cross at myself for being irritable. Jon's talk interrupted my thoughts *all* day and I was trying to think *out* of the gloom.

—Anne Morrow Lindbergh,
The Flower and the Nettle, 1976

The employed wife may be able with her earnings to buy labor-saving devices and the services of others. In addition she may have another, perhaps subtler resource: help from other members of the family. The fact that she works outside the home may give her leverage to call on them for help. . . . It appears that modern life has not shortened the woman's work day. Farm work has been greatly reduced, but it has been replaced by work in the labor force. Indeed, for married women in full-time jobs the work day is probably longer than it was for their grandmothers.

—Joann Vanek,
"Time Spent in Housework," 1974

If the floor needs washing, okay, I won't wash it, but I know it needs washing and it'll go on nagging me until I've washed it—so you can't win really.

—lorry driver's wife,
in Ann Oakley, *Woman's Work*, 1975

PEACEWORK
---

noun: a mental or spiritual act or condition marked by freedom from disquieting or oppressive thoughts or emotions.

May she become a flourishing hidden tree
That all her thoughts may like the linnet be,
And have no business but dispensing round
Their magnanimities of sound . . .

—W. B. Yeats,
"A Prayer for My Daughter," 1919

WOMAN'S WORK is piecework as well as peacework. Whoever she is and however she lives, somehow, sometimes, out of the fragments and ruins and the bits and pieces, in the edges and cracks of life, woman makes design.

[Madame Ratignolle] was very fond of Mrs. Pontellier, and often she took her sewing and went over to sit with her in the afternoons. . . . She had brought the pattern of the drawers for Mrs. Pontellier to cut out—a marvel of construction, fashioned to enclose a baby's body so effectually that only two small eyes might look out from the garment like an Eskimo's. . . .

—Kate Chopin, *The Awakening*, 1899

Sunday made her a very creditable and tolerably cheerful looking Mrs. Price, coming abroad with a fine family of children, feeling a little respite of her weekly cares. . . . Mrs. Price took her weekly walk on the ramparts every fine Sunday throughout the year, always going directly after morning service and staying till dinner-time. It was her public place; there she met her acquaintance, heard a little news, talked over the badness of the Portsmouth servants, and wound up her spirits for the six days ensuing.

—Jane Austen, *Mansfield Park*, 1814

Next Laura polished the stove with a flannel cloth, swept the floor, dropped the table leaf and spread a clean, bright red tablecloth over it. The cloth had a beautiful border and made the table an ornament fit for anyone's front room.

In the corner between the window to the east and the window to the south was a small stand-table with an easy armchair at one side and a small rocker at the other. Above it suspended from the ceiling was a glass lamp with glittering pendants. That was the parlor part of the room, and when the copies of Scott's and Tennyson's poems were on the stand it would be complete. She would have some geraniums growing in cans on the windows soon and then it would be simply beautiful.

—Laura Ingalls Wilder,
The First Four Years, 1971

. . . in the night, when my coughing was dry and tough, feet padded into the room, hands repinned the flannel, readjusted the quilt, and rested a moment on my forehead. So when I think of autumn, I think of somebody with hands who does not want me to die . . .

—Toni Morrison, *The Bluest Eye*, 1970

Once upon a time a woman had to give a party. Maybe she didn't want to but she certainly had to. The first thing she did in preparation for it was to have a sinking feeling in the pit of her stomach. But like every other hostess, she knew that it would

go away if she set to work. And work she did. And at many jobs. Whether she knew it or not she was, as she prepared for that party, alternately and sometimes simultaneously chief, cook, bottle-washer, mechanic, decorator, designer, nutritionist, economist, bottler, steward, accountant, cofferer, laundress, pastry chef, sauceman, parlormaid, ladies' maid, carver. And so she designed the party, always racing against the clock. And she was still racing in the final moments before the party. So the last cracker spread to be placed (at the last minute) beside the olives, the doorbell rings and she is still doing her hair, or changing her dress, or finding a pair of pantyhose without runs. Struggling between vanity and hospitality, she hesitates for just a second before the evening shift of work. She will be, before the night is out, once again many things: hostler, nanny (the children have to be disposed of somehow), diplomat, psychologist, sociologist, political scientist, valet, waitress, butler, powder room attendant, status seeker, fashion plate, siren, clean-up squad. In short, she will be the hostess.

But peace, of any sort, is hard work to negotiate. And sometimes the work that woman do doesn't work.

I used to work in television . . . [as] a producer's assistant for a programme called *Review of the Day.* . . .

My standards have definitely dropped since I've been doing housework all the time. I suppose it's because I really can't do anything uninterrupted and I still can't get used to that. It takes a lot of effort—like today, I woke up with a feeling, "I'm going to clean this place up." I always have great intentions at the beginning of the day, but by the end of it, just doing the routine things, I'm so fagged out I just collapse. Anyone listening to that recorder will probably think the place is a pigsty which, as you can see, it isn't. I'm very aware that there are little jobs I ought to do. I used to be pretty thorough and there are times when I think, "Oh I haven't got time to do that."

—"Juliet Warren," in Ann Oakley, *Woman's Work*, 1975

Women have no wilderness in them
They are provident instead,
Content in the tight hot cell of their hearts
To eat dusty bread.

They do not see cattle cropping red winter
    grass,
They do not hear
Snow water going down under culverts
Shallow and clear.

They wait, when they should turn to journeys
They stiffen, when they should bend
They use against themselves that benevolence
To which no man is friend.

They cannot think of so many crops to a
    field
Or of clean wood cleft by an axe.
Their love is an eager meaninglessness
Too tense, or too lax.

They hear in every whisper that speaks to
    them
A shout and a cry.
As like as not, when they take life over their
    door-sills
They should let it go by.

—Louise Bogan, "Women," 1953

Much is expected of the housewife, in that she should remain good-tempered, patient and calm amid the cares and worries of domestic life. Controlling a family with various temperaments, interests and problems, calls for great sympathy, affection and humour, and if to this is added the control of a domestic staff, with all the possibilities of temperamental clashes that this involves, it is obvious that a woman needs a considerable store of wisdom, inborn or acquired.

—Mrs. Beeton's
Cookery & Household Management, 1860

Later I throw up, and my mother says, "What did you puke on the bed clothes for? Don't you have sense enough to hold your head out the bed? Now, look what you did. You think I got time for nothing but washing up your puke?"

—Toni Morrison, *The Bluest Eye*, 1970

AND when the work doesn't work, and the pieces remain fragments, and the seams fall apart, every woman wants her mother, and the smell of somebody else's good cooking, and clean sheets on the bed.

Mama . . . Oh she was magic. If there were locks that were locked tight, she could get a little thing and open them. She could take old bent hangers and rags and make curtains and hang drapes. She ironed on chairs and made cakes every week and everybody loved her. Everybody."

—Lucille Clifton, *Generations*, 1976

We're mother and daughter
guests in a dark house
Our pictures are buried
in albums.

On this page
I'm gazing at you:
we no longer kiss,
my touch smears paint.

There's the snap of us,
you the bare-armed youth,
I a woman in muslin
crossing the tiles.

Then those cruel mouths
like broken clay,
eyes tagged fake,
ears for words that won't come.

Here's the one with the hat!
I (the antique in it's habitat)
lurking, yet brazen
and always there.
We shut the album on the mother
who's always crying,
always wild
with unrequited love.

—Estelle Leontief,
"Painting In Pompeii," 1976

GOOD WORKS

noun: an act or instance of deliberate generosity, a contribution made in a spirit of humanitarianism; an act or series of acts of aid to the needy.

BUT HOME is where you are, not any place you can go back to. And no matter how much you rub the brass genii's lamp with polish, no magic mother, no invisible peacemaker will appear. And who is to make the magic? You. How? Well, buy a hat, or a pair of shoes; have an argument or a joke—or a banana split. And often in times past, women would naturally turn to the community of women, would bathe themselves in the comfort, the balm, the oil, the musk, the unguents, the presence, the perfume, the sound, the touch, of other women.

In our time, both by choice and by chance women have sometimes severed themselves from the nourishment of the community of women. Like Ruth amid the alien corn, women follow after mobile husbands, or journey after their own jobs; older women who can, seek the sun; older women who can't, stay put in childless ghettos. But women don't know how much they know. So when women thirst, as they do, for other women, they once again, as in times past, re-create the community of women. Long-distance telephone calls, air mail letters, jet-span visits, koffee klatsches, consciousness-raising groups, women's studies programs, women's groups in this learned profession or that trade union guild—women once again reinforce, redesign, reassemble their efforts for the peaceful patchwork of their joined life.

Friday, April 26, 1935
Into town, lunch with Margot. We talked about the theory of having everything "emotionally real," "mean something." I think it is a rather silly theory. All relationships have to have commonplace bases. In marriage one can get it in something physical. . . . Relationships between women get the commonplace from those trivial femi-

nine things they have in common: hats and brassiere straps and children's problems, tomato juice and Haliver oil. I don't know what men get it from—all that business of smoking, drinking, and cussing the government.

—Anne Morrow Lindbergh,
Locked Rooms and Open Doors, 1974

IN OUR TIME, in our homes, in the new tasks and skills women increasingly attempt, women are more alone than they have ever been before. Prairie women on the Canadian plains, immigrant women in the ghettos of New York's East Side, women of every race and color and social class through history, surrounded willy-nilly by large families before there was the important revolution in contraceptive technology—women always had helping hands. A sociologist remainds us that

in the preindustrial home, there was no differentiation between cooking, eating and sitting rooms. The hall, that is the entrance to the home, was the centre of domestic activity: here the family cooked, ate their meals, and relaxed together. Under these circumstances, housework was not the isolated activity it now is. The absence of modern labour-saving devices may have added to household work, but the absence of the kitchen, for the mass of the population, ensured that housework remained integrated with the main work of the family. The making of clothes, and the preparation of food—items in the ordinary housewife's role—were part of a communal work-activity.

—Oakley, *Woman's Work*, 1975

AND by hook or by crook, women have always had someone to teach them woman's work. And someone else to help them do it. Today, because we are isolated from our community of helping hands, it's harder. If you work in a cafeteria today, you still have to come home and clean up someone else's mess, even if it's only the cat's. But in times past, women of various ranks and skills and stations had other hands. The medieval lady, for example, had a staff of servants, and the household steward

(in earliest times a man) to instruct her in the managerial arts of domestic science: how to keep a stern eye on expenditures, supplies, staff; how to organize daily routine whether at home, on a pilgrimage, or under enemy siege; how to give a good banquet—including the additional hay needed to feed her guests' horses. And not just in upper-class homes. Until well into the seventeenth century female apprentices learned trades and crafts from "ale wives" (brewing and a host of other skills belonged to women), and also learned the essentials of domestic responsibility. Lady of the manor or serving girl at the inn—women were tutored in the sciences and arts of homework; they learned to manage by doing.

Even as late as 1885, a Cambridge University professor's wife got by with the little help her husband could afford.

Dinner was at 7:45, and there were eight, nine, or even ten courses: I have some of the menus. Such dinners needed good organization, especially as they were all prepared and served by our own ordinary three servants, with very little extra help, beyond a waitress.

—Gwen Raverat, *Period Piece*, 1942

AN ambitious dinner party in that home—sometimes successful, sometimes not—might include:

Clear soup
Brill and lobster sauce
Chicken cutlets and rice balls
Oyster patties
Mutton, potatoes, artichokes, beets
Partridges and salad
Caramel pudding
Pears and whipped cream
Cheese ramequins
Cheese straws
Ices
Grapes, walnuts, chocolates and pears

Three servants didn't always ensure success, nor do twenty—but they helped.

Today, women's learning is not on-the-job training. How can it be, when there is so much we need to know that is new? Instead, women operate by laws rather than by lore—the cook goes to cooking classes, or watches the how-to of Chinese cooking on television; the crewel-worker turns to glossy pages of instruction in the women's magazines; the house cleaner imitates those wonder workers of the new technology in the TV advertisements; and all women must teach themselves many jobs, many skills. And more and more. When a woman works she is a multitude of workers: a nurse may be as well a wife, or a lover, an anxious mother, or dutiful daughter, a union member, a neighbor, a parishioner, a blood donor, a citizen, a poet.

But women manage, as they have always done. And what distinguishes women's management is that it seems to make room and corners, doors and recesses for unexpected tasks, tasks taken by choice. Women manage beyond the confines of the kitchen, beyond the combines of the field, factory, or the office, and somehow find the time to work some more—to entertain, to adorn, to instruct, and then with the time still remaining they pick up all their tools and do GOOD WORKS.

So I got a place in the factory of Hein & Fox. The hours were from 8AM to 6PM, and we made all sorts of linings—or, rather, we stitched in the linings-golf caps, yachting caps, etc. It was piece work, and we received from 3½ cents to 10 cents a dozen, according to the different grades. . . . After I had been working as a cap maker for three years it began to dawn on me that we girls needed an organization.

—Rose Schneidermann, "A Cap Maker's Story," *Independent*, April 27, 1905

What impact will rising unemployment have on volunteerism? Will the work of volunteers, many of whom put in 30 to 40 hours a week, threaten workers in paid jobs?

The seminar . . . also dealt with the feminist position that women should be paid for services, rather than donating them. . . .

"Volunteerism is simply a way you have of leading a double life," said Mrs. Jordan. She noted that . . . women could make a living in a field that satisfied most of their needs, but most people had still another side, with other talents and side interests.

Volunteer activities could utilize this other side."

—"In Light of Recession and Feminism, New Look at the Volunteer," *New York Times*, January 10, 1975

. . . in the new code of laws which I suppose it will be necessary for you to make, I desire you would remember the ladies and be more generous and favorable to them than your ancestors. Do not put such unlimited power into the hands of the husbands. Remember all men would be tryants if they could. If particular care and attention is not paid to the ladies, we are determined to foment a rebellion, and will not hold ourselves bound by any laws in which we have no voice or representation.

—Abigail Adams to John Adams, March 31, 1776

That same year Lady Mary Wortley Montagu contracted smallpox, to the ruin of her beauty. The following year her husband was sent as ambassador to the Turkish court in Constantinople. Lady Mary . . . was greatly impressed by what she saw of the Turkish practice of variolation. She had the embassy physician inoculate her young son, and on her return to London in 1718 she agitated enthusiastically in favor of variolation. . . . Lady Mary deserves great credit both for her courage in having her children inoculated and for her persistent propaganda in court circles.

—W. L. Langer, "Immunization against Smallpox before Jenner," *Scientific American*, January 1967

Born a slave in Ulster County, New York, Sojourner Truth . . . was sold four times in her first thirty years of life. The Abolition Law . . . freed her but was violated by her master, who sold her fifth child illegally. Her relentless struggle to recover her son brought her before the Grand Jury of New York where she won her case.

. . . she used the public platform to preach and teach abolitionism, equality of the races and sexes, temperance, prison reform. . . .

During the Civil War she met President Lincoln and urged him to enlist northern free black men to fight in the union armies. She remained in Washington . . . nursing the wounded soldiers and finding shelter and food for newly emancipated slaves. . . . At 70 she attended the Women's Rights Convention in New York in 1867 and warned the women to get going because she didn't intend to die until she voted.

—Wendy Martin,
The American Sisterhood, 1972

PATCHES OF HONOR

noun: an ornament, badge or tab of cloth sewed on a garment, an emblem worn at the shoulder of a military uniform to show the unit to which a serviceman belongs.

Mrs. Benson, an architect married to an architect (they both work at home), begins her description of a weekday thus:
    7:55 Remind son of time,
    8:45 Mend daughter's nightdress,
    9:15 Organize a party and the day's laundry,
    9:45 Go to shops, laundry, chemist— thread, plant, fish, buns, polish,
    11:05 Get office coffee, hang out day's laundry,
    11:40 Work finally started.
During the same period Mr. Benson got up at nine, read his mail, started his office work at ten, and worked through till lunch at one.

—Ann Oakley,
The Sociology of Housework, 1974

OFFICIAL WAR and its tactics have always been man's work. But women win stars, too. Who among women win medals, and for what? Well certainly the "firsts":

—Elizabeth Blackwell, the first woman physician in America;

—Madame Curie, the first woman to win a Nobel Prize for science;
—Amelia Earhart, the first woman to win the skies;
—and the first woman lawyer, woman architect, woman bus driver, woman riveter, woman tennis champ, woman jockey, woman minister, woman rabbi, woman president, woman astronaut . . .

Yes. But while those medals are rusting, the rest of us are out earning our own. For most of us, the war in which we will win our patches of honor is unofficial. We may fight in the public world but at the same time we are waging constant war in our houses, our bodies, ourselves.

The interviewing officer . . . stressed that if she agreed to his proposal [to become an undercover intelligence spy] she would not have the protection of a uniform, and that in the event of capture, she would be interrogated by the Gestapo—"something no human being could face with anything but terror" . . . He suggested that, as a writer and broadcaster, she might be useful to humanity again after the war. She was in contact with the minds of children who would have to live in a partially destroyed world. "It might seem academic, considering our desperate situation right now, but you should consider if you might be better employed rebuilding society."

—William Stevenson,
A Man Called Intrepid, 1976

. . . they were growing up. Even the baby was eight now. They had kept her so busy, worrying about them even when she wasn't with them had kept her so busy, guilt about them (not very profound, she had to admit) had occupied the surface reaches of her being with its endless little squalls and tempests, so that she had hardly had time to worry about herself. She had reeled from job to job, from country to country, . . . organizing meals and washing machines and schools and laundries, buying socks for Spike in Alexandria, rushing home from Glasgow to take Josh to the doctor about his balls, writing shopping lists even in the middle of lectures and seminars, consulting timetables, ringing stations, arranging fantastically elaborate schedules, shouting at domestic agencies, swearing at gasmen, bursting into tears one shaming day in front of her accountant because she'd left her bank statements in her lecture folder, never going to a hairdresser, wearing the same clothes till they fell to pieces, and listening to other people telling her how busy she must be till she believed it herself.

—Margaret Drabble,
The Realms of Gold, 1975

As THE counterattacks mount we demand the most sophisticated yet covert network of intelligence, a network whose central intelligence agency is the community of women. To wage successful campaigns in our lives, woman's strategy must of necessity be global—her battle plan must equip her to manage in the face of total war. So a woman may be flying high—as stewardess, or pilot, or bombardier—but then her child will fall sick, or there's an unexpected one growing in her stomach, or her necklace splatters over the controls, or she's left her pocketbook down on the ground in the ladies' room, or she's hoping that he'll wait at the hotel because she's already very late . . .

A woman's life is a squadron of operatives. She conducts—in her finest hours—an integrated intelligence unit. Her bold missions are to ensure survival—hers, that of her kins, her comrades (and enemies), her community. Unlike men, the skirmishes a woman fights are both public and private—a woman general seldom takes her helmet off, except to polish its brass fittings.

In Swiss valleys to-day the traveller comes sometimes on the figure of a solitary woman climbing the mountain-side, on her broad shoulders a mighty burden of fodder or manure she is bearing up for the cattle, or to some patch of cultivated land. . . . The face is seamed and seared with the stern marks of toil and endurance, as the mountain-side is with marks of storm and avalanche. It is the face of one who has brought

men into the world in labour and sorrow, and toiled mightily to sustain them. . . . the type of the mighty labouring woman who has built up life.

—Olive Schreiner,
Woman and Labour, 1911

AND though women don't make five-star general or admiral, most women experience the cross fire of one siege or another and then another; their working lives are made up of forays, which, with great courage and cunning, they can marshal into victories. And if alone, sequestered from the help and support of other women, commandeering only mechanical infantry—typewriters or washing machines, automobiles or hot combs—to implement stratagems, we do well to rally to the cries of the best generals among us. Their woman's wisdom is: Dignify every detail of the enterprise at hand. For there is honor as well as wisdom in what we know as women.

DEATH

The Last Mistress

BEFORE the ceremony of death unfolds, someone winds the winding sheet, someone wipes
the spittle and closes the eyes—"those are the
pearls that were his eyes"—someone straight-
ens the limbs and seals the lips. And then
tidies the room.

Astride of a grave and a difficult birth. Down in the hole, lingeringly, the grave-digger puts on the forceps.

—Samuel Beckett, *Waiting for Godot*, 1953

I was called in New York at four o'clock in the morning and told that my mother had died. After I got home, Mrs. McKirk took me aside and said, "What shall I do with the sheets? Should I put them in the wash or throw them out?—you know your mother bled to death." And I said, "Is the mattress ruined, because if it is, we'll have to get rid of it before Daddy comes home."

WOMEN labor to bear life; and labor to bear death as well.

While I was waiting, the child began to cry worse than ever before; she would not take the breast, and I could do nothing to soothe her, either by walking or resting, so that I was greatly troubled. At last the doctor came, and began to examine her; and in the same moment I noticed that her crying grew feebler, and that her lips were becoming paler and paler. Then, as I could not remain silent, seeing her thus, I had to ask, "How is her condition?" "She cannot live until evening," he answered. "But could you not give her medicine?" I asked. "If she could drink it," he replied.

I wanted to go back home at once, and send word to my husband and to my father's house; but the shock had been too much for me—all my strength had suddenly left me. Fortunately a kind old woman came to my aid, and carried my umbrella and other things, and helped me to get a jinrikisha, so that I was able to return home by jinrikisha. Then I sent a man to tell my husband and my father. Mita's wife came to help me; and with her assistance everything possible was done to help the child. . . . Still my husband did not come back. But all our pain and trouble was in vain.

So, on the second day of the fifth month of the thirty-second year, my child set out on her journey to the heaven of Amida— never to return to this world.

—unknown Japanese woman, "A Woman's Diary," 1898, from *Revelations: Diaries of Women*, edited by Mary Jane Moffat and Charlotte Painter

THE KINGDOM of death needs to be greeted as much as the manger of birth; and women housekeep and keep house here, too. Someone must.

The baby's body was found in the woods near the road from Hopewell to Princeton. It was identified by the homemade shirt Betty and I put on it. Also the teeth and hair. . . . I thought I would lead [my baby] and teach him and now he has gone first into the biggest experience in life. He is ahead of me. . . . Last night I went into his closet, opened the door, a flood of warmth. His blue coat on a hook, his red tam, his blue Dutch suit, the little cobweb scarf we tied around his neck. I opened the suitcase and went over each suit. His two wrappers hung on a hook and a pair of white shoes and his bunny bedroom boots. In the pockets of his blue coat I found a shell, a "tee," and his red mittens. It was like touching his hand. In the drawers I found all the Hansel and Gretel set he played with that last day and the little pussycat I pushed in and out of a little toy house for it. It delighted him so. It gave me a pang of happiness to find it again. Oh, it was good to feel that intimacy of that memory. It was grief; but it was my own boy—real, alive in my memory, not a police case. I gave Mother the shell and tee.

—Anne Morrow Lindbergh, *Hour of Gold, Hour of Lead, Diaries and Letters 1929–1932*, 1973

AND the closets of the dead, the drawers of the deceased, clothing, false teeth, eyeglasses, shoes, letters, medicines, rings, watches, coats —the paraphernalia of life—must be sorted and assigned.

WOMAN'S work is to mourn in the house of the dead, and to prepare the house of the dead for mourners.

You should have seen the food they had waiting for everybody back at the house. Cheeses, cakes, cucumber sandwiches, and thank goodness, lots of liquor. And her friends, even such fancy women in their skinny bodies, everyone of them brought a casserole, some cookies, one even came with a whole cooked ham with pineapple and cloves on the outside. And the eating . . . I can't tell you how proud Fanny would have been if she hadn't been busy pushing up daisies. And I told her daughters so. I was proud, too. Those girls sure know how to do things.

RARELY do women linger over their own deaths; they leave that to men who meditate as well upon the legacies of their lives. Man rages:

> Picture and book remain,
> An acre of green grass
> For air and exercise,
> Now strength of body goes;
> Midnight, an old house
> Where nothing stirs but a mouse.
>
> My temptation is quiet
> Here at life's end
> Neither loose imagination,
> Nor the mill of the mind
> Consuming its rag and bone,
> Can make the truth known.
>
> Grant me an old man's frenzy,
> Myself must I remake
> Till I am Timon and Lear
> Or that William Blake
> Who beat upon the wall
> Till Truth obeyed his call;
>
> A mind Michael Angelo knew
> That can pierce the clouds,
> Or inspired by frenzy
> Shake the dead in their shrouds;
> Forgotten else by mankind,
> An old man's eagle mind.

> —W. B. Yates, "An Acre of Grass," 1938

> Time held me green and dying,
> Though I sang in my chains like the sea.

> —Dylan Thomas, "Fern Hill," 1952

WOMAN keens.

Maurya [in a low voice, but clearly]. It's little the like of him knows of the sea. . . .

Bartley will be lost now, and let you call in Eamon and make me a good coffin out of the white boards, for I won't live after them. I've had a husband, and a husband's father, and six sons in this house—six fine men, though it was a hard birth I had with every one of them and they coming to the world—and some of them were found and some of them were not found, but they're gone now the lot of them. . . . There were Stephen and Shawn were lost in the great wind, and found after in the Bay of Gregory of the Golden Mouth, and carried up the two of them on one plank and in by that door. . . . There was Sheamus and his father, and his own father again, were lost in a dark night. . . . There was Patch after was drowned out of a curagh turned over. I was sitting here with Bartley, and he a baby lying on my two knees, and I seen two women, and three women, and four women coming in, and they crossing themselves and not saying a word. I looked out then, and there were men coming after them, and they holding a thing in the half of a red sail, and water dripping out of it—it was a dry day, Nora—and leaving a track to the door. . . .

> —J. M. Synge, *Riders to the Sea*, 1906

> I am a widow, alone and dressed in black,
> Simply wearing a sad face,
> In great pain and with a distressed manner
> I wear my very bitter mourning which kills me.
>
> Well I have reason to be completely overcome,
> Full of tears and scarcely able to speak;
> I am a widow, alone and dressed in black.
>
> Since I have lost the one for whom I continue
> To grieve to the point of madness,
> Farwell good times!
> My joy is gone, my good fortune fallen on hard times;
> I am a widow, alone and dressed in black.

> —Christine de Pisan, "Rondeau," 1429

> Queen Margaret . . . If ancient sorrow be most reverent,
> Give mine the benefit of seniory
> And let my griefs frown on the upper hand.

If sorrow can admit society,
Tell over your woes again by viewing mine.
I had an Edward, till a Richard killed him;
I had a Harry, till a Richard killed him;
Thou hadst an Edward, till a Richard killed
   him;
Thou hadst a Richard, till a Richard killed
   him . . .

—Shakespeare, *Richard III*, seventeenth
century

WOMEN live in the growing and grieving of
generations. They know that grief, good grief,
like moss upon stone buildings, grips yet
weathers human seasons. And it is for their
connectedness to life in death that women
grieve.

The sight of my mother's nakedness had
jarred me. No body existed less for me:
none existed more. As a child I had loved
it dearly; as an adolescent it had filled me
with an uneasy repulsion: all this was perfectly in the ordinary course of things and
it seemed reasonable to me that her body
should retain its dual nature, that it should
be both repugnant and holy—a taboo. But
for all that, I was astonished at the violence
of my distress. . . . this body, suddenly
reduced by her capitulation to bring a body
and nothing more, hardly differed at all from
a corpse—a poor defenceless carcass
turned and manipulated by professional
hands, one in which life seemed to carry
on only because of its own stupid mo-
mentum. For me, my mother had always
been there, and I had never seriously
thought that some day, that soon I should
see her go. Her death, like her birth, had
its place in some legendary time . . .

—Simone de Beauvoir, *A Very
Easy Death*, 1965

What youthful mother, a shape upon her
   lap
Honey of generation had betrayed,
And that must sleep, shriek, struggle to
   escape
As recollection or the drug decide,
Would think her son, did she but see that
   shape
With sixty or more winters on its head,

A compensation for the pang of his birth,
Or the uncertainty of his setting forth?

—W. B. Yeats, "Among School Children,"
1928

Thursday, Sept. 24.—This is the Journal of
misfortunes. Shelley writes; he reads "Oedi-
pus Tyrannus" to me. On Tuesday, September 22, he goes to Venice. On Thursday, I
go to Padua with Clare; meet Shelley there.
We go to Venice with my poor Clara, who
dies the moment we get there. Mr. Hoppner
comes, and takes us away from the inn to
his house.

—*Mary Shelley's Journal*, edited by
Frederick L. Jones, 1947

Then Marjorie arrived, with a letter from
Thomas's wife saying that Thomas had
died of blackwater in the Zambesi Valley.
. . . Martha had not gone to her mother that
night. Instead she sat with Thomas's wife's
letter in her hand, not thinking about
Thomas—for what was there to think? And
not crying over him either. And she certainly was not able to hear what he said.

—Doris Lessing, *Landlocked*, 1958

Phoebus, make haste, the day's too long, be
   gone;
The silent night the fittest time for moan.
But stay this once, unto my suit give ear,
And tell my griefs in either hemisphere;
And if the whirling of thy wheels don't
   drown'd
The woeful accents of my doleful sound,
If in thy swift carrier thou canst make stay,
I crave this boon, this errand by the way:
Commend me to the man more loved than
   life,
Shew him the sorrows of his widowed wife,
My dumpish thoughts, my groans, my brak-
   ish tears,
My sobs, my longing hopes, my doubting
   fears,
And if he love, how can he there abide?
My interest's more than all the world beside.

—Anne Bradstreet, "A Letter to
Her Husband," 1678

Seldom, except in books, do the dying utter
memorable words, see visions, or depart
with beautified countenances; and those

who have sped many parting souls know that to most the end comes as naturally and simply as sleep. As Beth had hoped, the "tide went out easily;" and in the dark hour before the dawn, on the bosom where she had drawn her first breath, she quietly drew her last, with no farewell but one loving look; one little sigh. With tears and prayers and tender hands, mother and sisters made her ready for the long sleep that pain would never mar again, seeing with grateful eyes the beautiful serenity that soon replaced the pathetic patience that had wrung their hearts so long . . .

> —Louisa May Alcott, *Little Women*, 1868–69

My man is a bone ringed with weed.
Thus it was on my bridal night:
That the sea, risen to a green wall
At our window, quenching love's new de-
    light,
Stood curved between me and the midnight
    call
Of him who said I was so fair
He could drown for joy in the salt of my
    hair.
We sail, he said,
Like the placid dead
Who have long forgotten the marriage-bed.
    On my bridal night
Brine stung the window.
Alas, on every night since then
These eyes have rained
For him who made my heart sing
At the lifting of the latch;
For him who will not come again
Weary from the sea.

The wave tore his bright flesh in her greed:
My man is a bone ringed with weed.

> —Brenda Chamberlain, "Lament," 1958

She came to him there, and beside her went an attendant carrying the boy in the fold of her bosom, a little child, only a baby, Hektor's son, the admired, beautiful as a star shining, whom Hektor called Skamandrios. . . . Hektor smiled in silence as he looked on his son, but she, Andromache, stood close beside him, letting her tears fall, And clung to his hand and called him by name and spoke to him: 'Dearest, your

own great strength will be your death, and you have no pity on your little son, nor on me, ill-starred, who soon must be your widow; for presently the Achaians, gathering together, will set upon you and kill you; and for me it would be far better to sink into the earth when I have lost you, for there is no other consolation for me after you have gone to your destiny—only grief; since I have no father, no honoured mother. . . . Hektor, thus you are father to me, and my honoured mother, you are my brother, and you it is who are my young husband. Please take pity upon me then, stay here on the rampart, that you may not leave your child an orphan, your wife a widow . . .

> —Homer, *The Iliad*

WITH POMP and flourish, men court death in battles—their last mistress; women turn to greet death like a sister. Thus the moments of their deaths are still and solemn.

On Monday, Dr. Fordyce forbad the child's having the breast and we therefore procured puppies to draw off the milk. This occasioned some pleasantry of Mary with me and the other attendants. Nothing could exceed the equanimity, the patience and affectionateness of the poor sufferer. . . . Wedneday was to me the day of greatest torture. . . . It was now decided that the only chance of supporting her through what she had to suffer was by supplying her freely with wine. This task was devolved upon me. . . . Seeing that every hope was extinct, I was very desirous of obtaining from her any directions, that she might wish to have followed after her decease. Accordingly, on Saturday morning, I talked to her for a good while of the two children. . . . she at length said, with a significant tone of voice, "I know what you are thinking of". . . . At six o'clock on Sunday morning, September the tenth, Mr. Carlisle called me from my bed to which I had retired at one, in conformity to my request, that I might not be left to receive all at once the intelligence that she was no more. She expired at twenty minutes before eight.

> —William Godwin, *Memoirs of the Author [Mary Wollstonecraft] of A Vindication of the Rights of Woman,* 1798

Because I could not stop for Death,
He kindly stopped for me;
The carriage held but just ourselves
And immortality . . .

—Emily Dickinson, 1890

Dearest,
I feel certain that I am going mad again.
I feel we can't go through another of those
terrible times. And I shan't recover this
time. I begin to hear voices, and I can't con-
centrate. So I am doing what seems the best
thing to do. You have given me the greatest
possible happiness. You have been in every
way all that anyone could be. I don't think
two people could have been happier till this
terrible disease came. I can't fight any
longer. I know that I am spoiling your life,
that without me you could work. And you
will I know. You see I can't even write this
properly. I can't read. What I want to say
is I owe all the happiness of my life to you.
You have been entirely patient with me
and incredibly good. I want to say that—
everybody knows it. If anybody could have
saved me it would have been you. Every-
thing has gone from me but the certainty
of your goodness. I can't go on spoiling
your life any longer.
I don't think two people could have been
happier than we have been.

V. [Virginia Woolf]

When I could not find her anywhere in
the house or garden . . . I felt sure that she
had gone down to the river. I ran across
the fields down to the river and almost immediately found her walking-stick lying
upon the bank. I searched for some time
and then went back to the house and in-
formed the police. It was three weeks before her body was found when some children saw it floating in the river.

—Leonard Woolf, *The Journey Not*
the Arrival Matters, 1969

Last night there were four Marys
This night there'll be but three,
There was Mary Beaton and Mary Seaton
And Mary Carmichael and me.

Last night I dressed Queen Mary,
And put on her brae silk gown,
But all the thanks I've gotten this night
Is to be hang-ed in Edinburgh town.

They'll tie a kerchief round my eyes,
They'll no let me see to dee,
And they'll never tell my father or mother
But that I'm away o'er the sea.

O little did my mother think
The day she cradled me
Of the lands I was to travel in
Or the death I was to dee.

Last night there were four Marys,
This night there'll be but three,
There was Mary Beaton and Mary Seaton,
And Mary Carmichael and me.

—"Ballad of Mary Hamilton"

She felt herself to be dying about half an
hour before she became tranquil and apparently unconscious. During that half
hour was her struggle, poor soul! she said
she could not tell us what she sufferd, tho
she complaind of little fixed pain. When I
asked her if there was any thing she
wanted, her answer was she wanted nothing but death & some of her words were
'God grant me patience, Pray for me oh
Pray for me.' Her voice was affected but
as long as she spoke she was intelligible.
. . . I returned about a quarter before six
& found her recovering from faintness &
oppression, she got so well as to be able to
give me a minute account of her seisure &
when the clock struck 6 she was talking
quietly to me. . . . From that time till half
past four, when she ceased to breathe, she
scarcely moved a limb. . . . There was nothing convulsed or which gave the idea of
pain in her look, on the contrary, but for
the continual motion of the head, she gave
me the idea of a beautiful statue. . . .

—letter from Cassandra Austen to
Fanny Knight on Jane Austen's
death, July 1817

When the queen's prayers were finished,
the executioners asked her as was customary, to forgive them in advance for bring-

ing about her death. Mary answered immediately: 'I forgive you with all my heart, for now I hope you shall make an end of all my troubles.' Then the executioners, helped by Jane Kennedy and Elizabeth Curle, assisted the Queen to undress. . . . Stripped of her black, she stood in her red petticoat and it was seen that above it she wore a red satin bodice, trimmed with lace, the neckline cut low at the back; one of the women handed her a pair of red sleeves, and it was thus wearing all red, the colour of blood . . . that the queen of Scots died. . . . All the time her belongings were being stripped from her, it was notable that the queen neither wept nor changed her calm and almost happy expression of what one observer called 'smiling cheer'. . . . It was the queen's women who could not contain their lamentations as they wept and crossed themselves and muttered snatches of Latin prayers. Finally Mary had to turn to them and, mindful of her promise to Shrewsbury that they would not weep aloud if they were admitted to the hall, she admonished them softly in French: *Ne crie point pour moi. J'ai promis pour vous . . .*' When the queen was lying there quite motionless, Bull's assistant put his hand on her body to steady it for the blow. Even so the first blow, as it fell, missed the neck and cut into the back of the head. The queen's lips moved, and her servants thought they heard the whispered words: 'Sweet Jesus.' The second blow severed the neck, all but the smallest sinew and this was severed by using the axe as a saw. It was about ten o'clock in the morning of Wednesday 8 February, the queen of Scots being then aged forty-four years old, and in the nineteenth year of her English captivity.

—Antonia Fraser, *Mary Queen of Scots*, 1969

WILLINGLY, women do the work that death demands. But gladly they perform those acts of faith which support the feats of their working lives. Their communal religion is the illumination of their diurnal lives: childbirth, courtship, seduction, education, decoration, determination. For each other they compose litanies. And some few ecstatic voices sing the songs of the life in death, of survival.

Hail Mary,
Full of Grace
The Lord is with thee
Blessed art thou among women
Blessed is the fruit of Thy womb, Jesus
Holy Mary, Mother of God
Pray for us sinners now
And at the hour of our Death.

Suffer hardships now, despising the world's prosperity, be now fellow of the cross, hereafter sharer of the kingdom. Steer across the ocean freighted with holiness, till you leave the bark and land in Sion. May Sion's heavenly castle with its beauteous halls be your home when the term of life is past. . . . Herrad, who through the grace of God is abbess of the church in the Hohenburg, here addresses the sweet maidens of Christ who are working as though in the vineyard of the Lord; may He grant grace and glory unto them.—I was thinking of your happiness when like a bee guided by the inspiring God I drew from many flowers of sacred and philosophic writing this book called the 'Garden of Delights'; and I have put it together to the praise of Christ and the Church, and to your enjoyment, as though into a sweet honeycomb. Therefore you must diligently seek your salvation in it and strengthen your weary spirit with its sweet honey drops. . . and you will safely pass through what is transitory, and secure great and lasting happiness . . .

—The nun Herrad, *Garden of Delights*, twelfth century

My daughter, come and sit beside me—the end is not far off—receive instruction more precious than jewels, profitable both for this world and the next. For man's life is but a vain shadow; yet if thou hold fast to the counsels of righteousness, thou wilt pass on to a better life hereafter.

—Mwana Kupona, nineteenth-century Swahili poet, *Poem of the Wifely Duty*, edited by Alice Werner, 1914

Swing low,
Sweet chariot,
Comin' for to carry me home. . . .

NIGHTTIME

My Own Wayfaring

When you are old and gray and full of sleep,
And nodding by the fire, take down this
  book,
And slowly read, and dream of the soft look
Your eyes had once, and of their shadows
  deep;

How many loved your moments of glad
  grace,
And loved your beauty with love false or
  true;
But one man loved the pilgrim soul in you,
And loved the sorrows of your changing
  face.

And bending down beside the glowing bars
Murmur, a little sadly, how love fled
And paced upon the mountains overhead
And hid his face amid a crowd of stars.

—W. B. Yeats, "When You Are Old"

I make this song about me full sadly
my own wayfaring. I a woman tell
what griefs I had since I grew up
new or old never more than now.
Ever I know the dark of my exile . . .
My lord commanded me to move my dwell-
      ing here.
I had few loved ones in this land
or faithful friends. For this my heart grieves.

   —"The Wife's Lament," c.900

A shaft of steel speared upward and Dori woke with a small cry. She had never felt anything like it. . . . She glanced at the small clock on the table beside her; it was ten after one. . . . Then she knew. The image told her. It had begun.

   She was wild with elation. She was to time the pains. . . . She looked again at the clock. The minute hand had scarcely left the ten-after position. . . . She closed her eyes thinking about it, thinking. For once somebody is going to describe it; I'm a writer, or I used to be a writer anyway, and I'm going to remember every bit of it so I can set it down for the record . . .

   —Laura Z. Hobson,
   The Tenth Month, 1970

The hands that felled trees also cut um-bilical cords; the hands that wrung the necks of chickens and butchered hogs also nudged African violets into bloom; the arms that loaded sheaves, bales, and sacks rocked babies into sleep. They patted biscuits into flaky ovals of innocence—and shrouded the dead. They plowed all day and came home to nestle like plums under the limbs of their men. The legs that straddled a mule's back were the same ones that straddled their men's hips.

   —Toni Morrison, *The Bluest Eye*, 1970

Sun and moon travelled on, and left her, passed her by, a rich woman enjoying her riches. . . .

   —D. H. Lawrence, *The Rainbow*, 1915

Five minutes later Diana was in her dressing-room, where she wrote at night, on the rare occasions now when she was left free for composition. Beginning to dwell on THE MAN OF TWO MINDS, she glanced at the woman likewise divided, if not similarly; and she sat brooding . . .

   —George Meredith,
   Diana of the Crossways, 1885

Pain penetrates

Me drop
by drop

   —Sappho, Fragment 61

Sometimes I feel like
Like a motherless child
A long way from home.

Hush little baby
Don't say a word . . .

I hate to see that evenin' sun go down.

Come to me, quietly
Do not do me injury.
Gently, Johnny,
My jingalo.

At midnight tears
Run into your ears.

   —Louise Bogan, "Solitary
   Observations Brought Back from
   a Sojourn in Hell," 1954

Sleep, darling

I have a small
daughter called
Cleis, who is

like a golden
flower
         I wouldn't
take all Croesus'
kingdom with love
thrown in, for her

   —Sappho, Fragment 17

ALONE at night I am many things. I undress. My shoes go first and that feels good. And then my dress. I am fewer things now. But without that uniform, I'm more alone; more me. My face. I take it off too. I see myself, I worry, I mourn, I even weep. But I'm in my underwear. I've got to get it off too. And what I want to do is rip these things that bind and strain and chafe. Stripped now, I really see myself, I'm surprised. And then I take nighttime on, and like the moon, I become Our Lady of Perpetual Sorrow. I am alone. And fear comes. Shadows, shades, wraiths, demons, monsters touch me. I turn on the other light. I steady myself. Will I rest tonight before I sleep? I'm soothed, sleepy too. Sleepier still, as I lull myself to sleep. Snatches of womantalk . . . womansong . . . womanwork . . . never done.

ABOUT THE AUTHORS

GINA LURIA is the editor of an 89-volume reprint series on the *Feminist Controversy 1788-1810*. She received her Ph.D. in English from New York University and is a scholar at Pforzheimer Library. Dr. Luria has written on the problems of Wollstonecraft scholarship in several scholarly journals as well as position papers in women's studies. Formerly on the faculty of Rutgers University, where she was the director of Women's Studies, she now lives in Chicago with her husband and son.

VIRGINIA TIGER, author of *William Golding: The Dark Fields of Discovery* (1975), is an associate professor in the Department of English at Rutgers University and the director of Women's Studies there. She is a graduate of the University of Toronto and the University of British Columbia, where she received her Ph.D. Dr. Tiger, a Canadian, lives in New York City with her husband, the anthropologist Lionel Tiger, and their son.